PEOPLE
IN THE NEWS

Robin Williams

by John F. Wukovits

LUCENT
BOOKS®

THOMSON
━━━━★━━━━ ™
GALE

San Diego • Detroit • New York • San Francisco • Cleveland
New Haven, Conn. • Waterville, Maine • London • Munich

THOMSON

GALE ™

On cover: Robin Williams is photographed at the 2003 Golden Globe awards.

To my daughter, Karen, whose accomplishments have made me smile

LIBRARY OF CONGRESS CATALOGING-IN-PUBLICATION DATA

Wukovits, John F., 1944-
    Robin Williams / by John F. Wukovits.
        p. cm. — (People in the news)
    Summary: Profiles comedian and actor Robin Williams, whose award-winning career includes stand-up comedy work, the television series "Mork and Mindy," and movies such as "Mrs. Doubtfire" and "Aladdin."
    Includes bibliographical references and index.
    ISBN 1-56006-778-0 (hardback : alk. paper)
    1. Williams, Robin, 1952 July 21—Juvenile literature. 2. Actors—United States—Biography—Juvenile literature. 3. Comedians—United States—Biography—Juvenile literature. [1. Williams, Robin, 1952 July 21– 2. Comedians. 3. Actors and actresses.]
    I. Title. II. People in the news (San Diego, Calif.)
    PN2287.W473W85 2004
    791.43'028'092—dc21
                                                                    2003006838

Printed in the United States of America

Table of Contents

Foreword   4

Introduction
"This Might Be the One Time I'm Speechless"   6

Chapter 1
Comedy Was a Way of Connecting   11

Chapter 2
"This Kid Is Going to Make It"   23

Chapter 3
"I Knew I Could Make These People Laugh"   33

Chapter 4
"I Am Mork from Ork"   44

Chapter 5
The Deadly Sins of Hollywood Wait for Everyone   57

Chapter 6
"Accomplished and Familiar as an Actor"   69

Chapter 7
"He's Loved Even When He's Not Being Funny"   80

Notes   93
Important Dates in the Life of
   Robin Williams   97
For Further Reading   101
Works Consulted   103
Index   106
Picture Credits   111
About the Author   112

Foreword

Fame and celebrity are alluring. People are drawn to those who walk in fame's spotlight, whether they are known for great accomplishments or for notorious deeds. The lives of the famous pique public interest and attract attention, perhaps because their experiences seem in some ways so different from, yet in other ways so similar to, our own.

Newspapers, magazines, and television regularly capitalize on this fascination with celebrity by running profiles of famous people. For example, television programs such as *Entertainment Tonight* devote all of their programming to stories about entertainment and entertainers. Magazines such as *People* fill their pages with stories of the private lives of famous people. Even newspapers, newsmagazines, and television news frequently delve into the lives of well-known personalities. Despite the number of articles and programs, few provide more than a superficial glimpse at their subjects.

Lucent's People in the News series offers young readers a deeper look into the lives of today's newsmakers, the influences that have shaped them, and the impact they have had in their fields of endeavor and on other people's lives. The subjects of the series hail from many disciplines and walks of life. They include authors, musicians, athletes, political leaders, entertainers, entrepreneurs, and others who have made a mark on modern life and who, in many cases, will continue to do so for years to come.

These biographies are more than factual chronicles. Each book emphasizes the contributions, accomplishments, or deeds that have brought fame or notoriety to the individual and shows how that person has influenced modern life. Authors portray their subjects in a realistic, unsentimental light. For example, Bill Gates—the cofounder and chief executive officer of the software giant Microsoft—has been instrumental in making personal computers the most vital tool of the modern age. Few dispute his business savvy, his perseverance, or his technical expertise, yet critics say he is ruthless in his dealings with competitors and driven more by his desire to maintain Microsoft's dominance in the computer industry than by an interest in furthering technology.

In these books, young readers will encounter inspiring stories about real people who achieved success despite enormous obstacles. Oprah Winfrey—the most powerful, most watched, and wealthiest woman on television today—spent the first six years of her life in the care of her grandparents while her unwed mother sought work and a better life elsewhere. Her adolescence was colored by promiscuity, pregnancy at age fourteen, rape, and sexual abuse.

Each author documents and supports his or her work with an array of primary and secondary source quotations taken from diaries, letters, speeches, and interviews. All quotes are footnoted to show readers exactly how and where biographers derive their information and provide guidance for further research. The quotations enliven the text by giving readers eyewitness views of the life and accomplishments of each person covered in the People in the News series.

In addition, each book in the series includes photographs, annotated bibliographies, timelines, and comprehensive indexes. For both the casual reader and the student researcher, the People in the News series offers insight into the lives of today's newsmakers—people who shape the way we live, work, and play in the modern age.

Introduction

"This Might Be the One Time I'm Speechless"

IN MANY WAYS, Robin Williams reached the pinnacle of success on the strength of his enormous talents. During a performing career that began in 1977 and incorporated stage, film, and television, he had compiled an impressive array of awards and critical acclaim, many rolling in because of his razor-sharp wit. By the year 1997, he could look back with pride at his vast accomplishments—thirty-three motion pictures, four Grammy Awards for comedy recordings, five Golden Globe Awards, two Emmy Awards, and fame as the star of one of the nation's top-rated television situation comedies.

That might have been enough for most people, but one glaring omission bothered Robin Williams. Despite three Academy Award nominations for acting, he had been passed over each time—once in 1988, again in 1990, and another time in 1992. It seemed that the Academy voters, his fellow actors who each year selected the recipients of Hollywood's most revered honor, had continued a pattern that had existed since Oscar's earliest days— that of ignoring individuals whose roots began with comedy. Academy voters through the years had denied the Oscar to comedians, as if to convey that only those actors with serious training in drama should be considered for the honor. As a result, even a performer as heralded as Charlie Chaplin had waited an entire career without clutching the cherished gold Oscar statuette.

This issue bothered Williams because, unknown to a great many in the general public, he had actually entered acting with the intention of becoming a serious dramatic actor. Only when he failed to find work in that field did he turn to comedy as his prime occupation. Despite that, he considered himself gifted in serious roles, a fact supported by his three Academy Award nominations. And he wondered if he would ever have the chance to

Awards for Robin

Robin Williams has collected many awards throughout his distinguished career, among them one of the performing industry's highest honors, the Academy Award. Even if Williams had not taken home a coveted Oscar for *Good Will Hunting,* however, he could look back with satisfaction at a job well done. Some of the major awards he has received include the following:

Academy Award

1998—Academy Award as best supporting actor, *Good Will Hunting*

Emmy Award

1987—Emmy Award for outstanding individual performance in a variety or musical program, "A Carol Burnett Special"

1988—Emmy Award for outstanding individual performance in a variety or musical program, "ABC Presents a Royal Gala"

Golden Globe Award

1979—Golden Globe Award for best actor in a television comedy series, *Mork and Mindy*

1988—Golden Globe Award for best actor for a musical or comedy, *Good Morning, Vietnam*

1992—Golden Globe Award for best actor for a musical or comedy, *The Fisher King*

1992—Golden Globe Award for special achievement, *Aladdin*

1993—Golden Globe Award for best actor in a comedy, *Mrs. Doubtfire*

Grammy Awards

1979—Grammy Award for best comedy recording, *Reality . . . What a Concept*

1987—Grammy Award for best comedy recording, *A Night at the Met*

1988—Grammy Award for best comedy recording, *Good Morning, Vietnam*

1988—Grammy Award for best children's recording, *Pecos Bill*

lift the Oscar statuette and bask in the adulation of his fellow performers, not because he made them laugh but because he moved
them with his dramatic talents.

"Let's See Some I.D."

A pair of young writers handed Williams the vehicle with which
he was to achieve his elusive goal. Matt Damon, age twenty-eight,
and his lifelong friend from Boston, Ben Affleck, age twenty-six,
had cowritten a powerful script about a troubled mathematical genius from a rough Boston neighborhood who finds help from a
community college professor of psychology, himself plagued with
personal demons. Together, mainly through discussions in the professor's office, the two work through their various problems.

At first, Robin Williams could not believe that such a powerful script could have been penned by two such inexperienced authors. When he met the duo for the first time and saw how young
they actually looked, Williams blurted out, "Let's see some I.D.,"[1]
as if to indicate that the two were not even old enough to legally
consume alcoholic beverages. The screenwriters were not dis-
suaded, however, as they had had Robin Williams in mind for the
professor when they wrote the script.

Williams instantly accepted the role as the professor. The story
appealed to him. He loved the manner in which both characters
in the film turn to one another for help and thus become better
individuals.

One of the film's most dramatic scenes took place on a Boston
park bench, where the troubled genius, portrayed by Matt Damon,
listens as Robin Williams's professor explains to him why, even
though he may be a genius, he actually knows nothing of life. The
extraordinary four-minute monologue captivated audiences, as
Robin Williams delivered a string of powerful lines about his character's experiences. He spoke about his character's time in
Vietnam and the loss of his wife, not in an angry way but with a
quiet acceptance that what happened was out of his control and
that only the future could be affected by his actions.

In early 1998, Williams was rewarded for this performance
with his fourth Academy Award nomination, but he faced the out-
come with bittersweet resignation. Certainly, the nod pleased

Robin Williams counsels a troubled Matt Damon in the 1997 film Good Will Hunting.

Williams, but he wondered whether he would ever overcome the voters' bias against comedians winning for dramatic roles.

On top of that, he faced stiff competition for the award, especially from actor Burt Reynolds, who gained rave notices for his performance in *Boogie Nights*. The two split the acting competitions that preceded the Oscars. Reynolds took the Golden Globe, and Williams captured the Screen Actors' Guild Award for best supporting actor.

When the night of the Oscar presentation arrived on March 23, 1998, Reynolds and Williams appeared to be the cofavorites to win, but neither could rest easily. Academy voters have a history of tossing in surprises. Anyone in the category could win, especially noted actor Anthony Hopkins for *Amistad* and Greg Kinnear for *As Good As It Gets*.

On Oscar night, Williams waited anxiously as the presenter opened the envelope containing the name of the winner. When he heard his name, a stunned Williams hugged his wife, Marsha, and

Williams accepts an Oscar for his portrayal of a psychology professor in Good Will Hunting. *Williams became the first comedian to win an Academy Award.*

then rushed onstage where his longtime friend and fellow comedian, Oscar host Billy Crystal, waited with a huge smile. "Ah, man! This might be the one time I'm speechless,"[2] proclaimed an unbelieving Williams.

In the rest of his brief speech, he credited the people who had helped him achieve such success. He thanked his wife, Marsha, "the woman who lights my soul on fire every morning,"[3] mentioned he still wanted to see some identification from Matt Damon and Ben Affleck, and then raised his statuette toward the heavens in a nod to his late father, Robert. Then, Williams walked off stage with the one item no other comedian in the long history of film had ever gained—an Oscar.

An ebullient Williams later explained that he considered his chances of winning very poor. "I didn't think I had a chance, and when they said it [announced his name as winner], I was shocked. This is a wild night. It's just insane. I'm very proud. This is an extraordinary piece and the first time I read it I wanted to do it."[4]

Robin Williams's journey from gifted comedian to Oscar-winning dramatic actor had followed a winding, sometimes tortuous route that included both happiness and sorrow. During his time as a youth and as an adult, he enjoyed love while enduring isolation, experienced rejection while basking in acceptance, gained fame while wallowing in the costs that come with it.

Chapter 1

Comedy Was a Way of Connecting

UNIQUE IS ONE word that many people associate with Robin Williams. But like every other individual, he alone cannot take credit for his amazing array of talents and personality traits. He developed them to the degree that has made him famous, but he also acknowledges that the traits and values were, in part, handed down from his parents, a remarkable couple who, while appearing to have little in common, actually molded a strong marriage that spanned decades. It was from these individuals that Robin Williams received the foundation upon which he, through dint of creativity and hard work, then fashioned his career.

A Stern Father

Born July 21, 1952, in Chicago, Illinois, Robin McLaurim Williams was named for the title character in Marjorie Haynes's children's book, *Robin on the River*. His father, Robert Fitzgerald Williams, was a senior executive with Ford Motor Company. A no-nonsense man who took immense pride in his work, Robert Williams studied problems with intensity, determined solutions, then doggedly insisted that the remedies be followed until the problem was eliminated.

He could be as autocratic at home. Robin claimed that his father, whom he always addressed as "Sir," reminded him of a retired English army colonel—proper, prim, and dutiful. Robin loved calling him "Lord Stokesbury, Viceroy of India," although not to his face, and sometimes found it awkward as a youth to feel close to the man. A large age gap—Robert was fifty years old at the time of Robin's birth—added to the difficulties of communication. Robin recalled the time when, as an eight year old, he brought home a report card of straight A's, confident of gaining his father's praise. The restrained man gazed at the report card and said in a calm voice, "Well done, son. Now, let's get ready for dinner."[5]

Despite this lack of emotion and active involvement from his father, who was also often away from home on business, Robin deeply respected the man. Williams has always claimed that his father served as an excellent role model who helped him develop a sense of values, common sense, and propriety. He never doubted that his father loved him, and other than one time, when Robin made a rude gesture to his mother, Robert never raised his voice to his son.

From his father, Robin also absorbed the ability to see the world through cautious, almost cynical, eyes. This trait Robin contends arose from his father's involvement in the brutally competitive automotive industry. "He was this wonderful elegant man who thought the world was going to hell in a hand basket," said Robin. "It was basically, 'You can't trust them. Watch out for them. They'll nail ya. Everybody's out to nail ya.'"[6] He tried to inculcate in his son the ability to judge people's intentions and to plan accordingly. In that manner, Robert believed, one avoided some of the unpleasant surprises that stand in wait along the path of life.

Robin McLaurim Williams was born in Chicago, Illinois (pictured). Williams credits his parents with instilling in him the values that helped bring him success.

Williams, pictured here performing with fellow comedian Billy Crystal, got his offbeat sense of humor from his mother, Laurie.

"A Crazy Southern Belle"

While words like "restrained," "cultured," and "refined" describe Robin's father, a different set of adjectives apply to his mother, Laurie, a former model. Robin called her "a crazy Southern belle"[7] who loved nothing more than a good joke or prank.

She once attended an exclusive dance at a very elegant tennis club, wearing an exquisite dress. When other ladies drew closer to her, however, and saw Laurie smile, they were stunned to see two teeth missing. As a joke, Robin's mother had stuck black chewing gum over her two front teeth to make it appear they had been knocked out. While she enjoyed laughing over the incident, some of the more refined women failed to grasp the humor and whispered to one another why anyone with such a wonderful taste in clothes could not afford to have her teeth fixed. "I got her energy and funkified sense of humor," said Robin, "and I got a ground-ing thing from Dad."[8]

Laurie Williams agreed that of the two parents, she was the more easygoing. "His dad was a disciplinarian; I was the pal."[9] But even that affords an inaccurate view of the situation. As the wife of a prominent Ford executive, Laurie Williams attended fre-quent society and charity functions, leaving the grade-school-age Robin home alone on many days.

"They'd Nail Me As Soon As I Got Through the Door"

While many children have tenuous relationships with their par-ents, some are able to alleviate the problem by turning to broth-ers and sisters. Here, too, Robin suffered a gap, as he had none with whom to share a childhood. Both parents had a son from a previous marriage—Todd Williams was thirteen years older than Robin, and McLaurin Smith was four years older—but the two lived with their other parent and rarely saw Robin.

He gained some comfort from school, but the diminutive, shy Williams experienced difficulty fitting in. He attempted to enter-tain friends from Gorton Elementary School in Chicago by mak-ing strange animal-like noises, but all it succeeded in doing was irritating his teacher, who often resorted to moving Robin's desk into the hallway.

Most classmates either ignored Williams or taunted him for being short, overweight, and withdrawn. Many mornings Williams walked into his public school, only to have the bigger students call him "leprechaun" or "dwarf" or beat him up. Williams turned to humor to deflect the name-calling, but this worked only part of the time. He later claimed that he first performed as an enter-tainer in the seventh grade, when he told jokes "as a way to keep from getting the shit kicked out of me. . . . They'd nail me as soon as I got through the door."[10]

Williams endured the teasing as well as he could, but the bit-ter treatment left scars that remain to the present day. Years later, after Robin had experienced drug abuse, the death of his father, and the breakup of his first marriage, a reporter asked him to re-late the most painful experience of his life. The entertainer selected none of the maladies that afflicted him as an adult. Instead, he recounted his elementary school and junior high years, when he frequently raced home with tears in his eyes.

A New School

Robin's life slowly began to change when he was twelve and the Ford Motor Company transferred his father to the Detroit, Michigan, area. Instead of heading to the public schools as he had done previously, Robin entered one of the most exclusive private institutions in the nation—the all-boys Country Day School in the wealthy Detroit suburb of Bloomfield Hills, home to many high-ranking auto executives.

Here, too, he at first found abuse. In addition to being short, overweight, and shy, Williams also felt the barbs of his classmates for wearing glasses. The other students considered him an outsider—Country Day was his sixth school in eight years due to his father's frequent moves around Chicago and Detroit. They also believed the quiet youth lacked intelligence because he rarely spoke. "I was picked on not only physically but intellectually, too,"[11] explained Williams.

Williams dealt with the scorn in the simplest way he knew— by avoiding it as much as possible. At the end of each school day, he sped back to the enormous thirty-room mansion that stood on

My Friend, the Dog

Robin Williams spent hours alone in his immense family mansion in Bloomfield Hills, Michigan, mainly as a defense against the teasing he experienced at school. The refuge provided by his home also handed the young boy training in using his imagination. For companionship, he often turned to his pet dog. Robin Williams explained those days to writer Lawrence Linderman in an interview with *Playboy* magazine.

I got started kind of early in floating and finding stuff to do. For instance, I made up my own little friends. [*In a child's voice*] "Can I come out and play?" "I don't know; I'll have to ask myself." We had a wonderful dog named Duke that would play hide-and-seek with me, and I could always find Duke, who thought that if he couldn't see me, I couldn't see *him*. Duke was dumb; I'd always spot—or hear—this big tail going *whop! whop! whop!* on the parquet floors.

twenty acres of land in Bloomfield Hills. But because his parents were so involved in their own activities and because no other children lived near his home, he had to occupy his time alone. "I was living on this huge estate. It was *miles* to the next kid," [12] Williams mentioned later.

"My Imagination Was My Friend"

With little alternative but to entertain himself, Williams turned to the talent that later gained him so much acclaim—his imagination. In the vast third floor of the mansion, which became his own private domain, Williams accumulated an immense collection of thousands of toy soldiers. With his dog, Duke, and his pet turtle, Carl, as his only companions, he spent hours arranging and re-arranging his medieval knights, Civil War cavalry, and World War II infantry to recreate titanic clashes. Gradually, he bestowed on many of the metallic soldiers their own voices and mannerisms and then enacted battles complete with shouts and sounds, orders and counterorders. Williams orchestrated the immense conflicts as if directing an epic movie, rapidly switching voices as he shuttled the toy soldiers from one part of the battlefield to another. "I would have time-machine battles with Confederate soldiers fighting GI's [World War II American infantry] with automatic weapons and knights fighting Nazis." [13] For a time, Williams cov-

An only child with no friends, Robin spent hours alone staging dramatic scenes with his toy soldiers.

ered a three-by-ten-foot wooden board with sand to recreate the World War II struggle for Guadalcanal.

These quiet moments spent alone helped develop the razor-sharp wit and incredible array of characterizations that Williams used to fashion an entertainment career. "My imagination was my friend, my companion,"[14] Williams said of his school years. That same imagination would later earn him praise and a handsome lifestyle.

A Talent for Mimicry

By age twelve Williams added another talent to his arsenal—the ability to mimic people around him. He loved to entertain his mother when they went food shopping by standing in the check-out line and imitating people waiting near them. After party guests departed the Williams mansion, Robin delighted his parents by perfectly recreating the voices and mannerisms of the individuals. Williams also studied television comedians of his day and adapted some of their techniques into his own "performances." He especially enjoyed the crazed antics of a performer named Jonathan Winters, a man who loved to create unique characters and voices for his sketches.

In a way, Williams was relying on his sense of humor and talent for mimicry to gain attention from his frequently absent parents. He said, "I performed for my parents as a way of saying, 'Love me.'"[15]

Williams later attributed his loneliness as a child and his attempts to gain notice as the springboard from which his career developed. With few friends to turn to, he developed his imagination and humor, then used that as a way of gaining acceptance. "My childhood was kind of lonely. Quiet," said Williams. "My father was away, my mother was working, doing benefits. I was basically raised by this maid, and my mother would come in later, you know, and I knew her and she was wonderful and charming and witty. But I think maybe comedy was part of my way of connecting with my mother. I'll make Mommy laugh, and that'll be okay, and that's where it started."[16]

Despite the lack of attention at home and the abuse at school, Williams does not regret his years as a youth. "I had a wonderful

The Origins of Comedy

Some people land in a certain profession by chance, others because they planned each step along the way. Although he refined his career path to varying degrees, Robin Williams was one of those youngsters who seemed to know what he wanted to do at a very early age. He once discussed his comedy roots with writer Lisa Grunwald from *Esquire* magazine. "Maybe it started off that I wanted the attention from mother, but it was also—I could do something here. Comedy is something I was meant to do, whether it's that kind of divine purpose or not. I was meant to do this [comedy]. I was not meant to sell insurance."

childhood. All I suffered from was a lack of a lot of parental contact. . . . There may have been some uncomfortable moments, but no anger or bitterness."[17]

A Turn to Sports

Sooner or later, an individual must decide either to allow events to drift along and let them influence him or to seize control and direct the path he takes. For Robin Williams, that decision came during his freshman year at Country Day School. Tired of existing on the outer fringes of school society, Williams decided to work out, lose weight, and join the wrestling team. Amazingly, the student who earlier showed little interest in sports quickly excelled in a demanding discipline. By the end of his freshman wrestling season, Williams registered an unbeaten record in league meets. He then reached the state finals in his weight class before losing to a more experienced opponent.

A dislocated shoulder ended Williams's chance to pursue wrestling in his sophomore year, so he switched to football that fall. However, at 103 pounds, Williams was much smaller than the other players, and he lasted barely one week. However, he ended the experience with the sense of humor that would mark his later years. William explained,

> They put me in at safety, and in my one and only scrimmage, the other squad ran every offensive play at me and over me. It was not easy for a 103-pound safety to stop a 200-pound running back. Toward the end of the practice, when the coach told me to get back in there, I asked him

if he'd mind painting me white so that I could disguise myself as a yard marker. [18]

Opting for activities that might be less likely to result in injury, Williams joined the soccer and track teams and enjoyed a measure of success, not only on the sports fields but in the social and scholastic arenas as well. Fellow students finally noticed the keen wit and the arsenal of characters that bounced around inside Williams's fertile mind. The once-reclusive teenager consequently found others drawing closer to him.

A Good Student

In high school, Williams tried to keep his social antics separate from the academic world. As a student, he maintained a serious demeanor and recorded impressive grades. He might quietly delight a few students with subtle comments or mimicry when no teacher was around, but once an adult walked near, he was quiet.

The serious student performed so ably in the classroom that in his junior year, he gained entrance to Country Day's exclusive Magna Cum Laude Society, a group of high-achieving upperclassmen.

Like these boys, Williams joined the wrestling team in high school. Success in sports and academics won him many friends.

Williams started thinking of his future and set his sights on entering an Ivy League college such as Princeton or Yale. The rejuvenated Williams had become so popular that he even considered running for class president his senior year.

As had happened so frequently in his life, however, Williams was again uprooted and placed in a different school when his father left the automotive industry and relocated in Tiburon, California, north of San Francisco. After many stressful years in a high-powered job, Robert Williams decided to retire. He believed that the automotive industry no longer cared about creating the best cars possible but was driven only by sales figures and by defeating the opposition. The elder Williams often returned home after long days on the job, looking exhausted. He explained to his disappointed son, "I loved what I did, but all they [Ford Motor Company] wanted to do was churn out as many cars as they could. The companies were losing their sense of pride in their product. I couldn't stand by and watch it happen. I had to get out." [19]

Though Robin Williams at first saw only that he was once again torn from familiar surroundings, the move to California proved to be one of the most crucial of his life. Because of his father's decision, the high school senior entered a radically different world than the ones he had known. The experience would unleash a transformed Robin Williams.

The New Kid in the Neighborhood

Since his father frequently had to move as a result of his job, Robin Williams experienced the difficulty of entering a new school—not once but over and over. In the book *Robin Williams* by Andy Dougan, Williams explained the effects of that experience.

> I was always being the new kid in the neighborhood. And since I was suffering from a case of the terminal shy I couldn't make friends that easily, and I always spent a lot of time in my room and I created my own little world full of all these little characters that had strange and unusual qualities. After a while, I realized that people found these characters funny and outrageous, and then it got to the point where I realized the characters could say and do things that I was afraid to do. And after a while, here I am.

"I Guess We Won't Be Speaking Latin Here"

In the summer of 1968, the Williams family packed their belongings and drove across country to Tiburon. The wealthy, quiet residential suburb was eighteen miles north of San Francisco, one of the nation's most vibrant cities and the scene of a burgeoning comedy community.

The first thing Robin Williams noticed about California was the fog. As the family drove by San Francisco toward Tiburon for the first time, dense fog rolled in quickly over the hills. A frightened Robin at first wondered if it was poison gas.

More startling changes occurred when Robin walked through the doors of his new school, Redwood High in Tiburon. Instead of wearing coats and ties, which Country Day required, students bounded about Redwood's hallways in beach gear and sandals. And female students, not allowed at the all-boys academy, freely walked in and out of classes.

When he examined the school's list of subject offerings, Williams received another shock. Instead of the Latin and medieval studies with which he had become accustomed in Michigan, he now stared at classes in filmmaking and black culture. Some teachers, dressed as casually as their students, halted classes to gather the students for what they called an energy hug. Williams explained later that entering Redwood High "changed me, [going] from this private school which was very rigid to this full-out crazy school which was amazing. I thought, 'This is certainly different. I guess we won't be speaking Latin here." [20]

Williams quickly adapted to the new lifestyle. He ditched the briefcase that had always accompanied him to Country Day and began wearing Hawaiian shirts and sandals to class. He soon had a bevy of new friends, every one drawn by the outrageous humor and creative wit of the new student from Michigan.

The California school also introduced Williams to a new and dangerous world—the drug scene. Students at Country Day drank alcohol, and some undoubtedly experimented with illegal substances, but drugs seemed to flourish among the students at Redwood High. "It was incredible to go from a private all-boys' high school to a place where . . . kids were always flying around on acid," Williams said in a magazine interview. "The first time I

Drug use was prevalent at Williams's California high school. There, Williams was exposed to the drug scene for the first time in his life.

walked into one of the bathrooms, a bunch of guys were in there, all spaced out. One kid took me aside and whispered, 'Don't wake them.' I didn't." [21]

Williams could not help but be influenced by the vast differences—in climate, in student behavior, in structure. He claimed that the drastic dissimilarities caused him to examine things from an entirely new perspective. Instead of the conservative, cautious approach with which Williams had been raised, he now examined concepts and attitudes through a more open, and in his case, liberating, filter.

Following the routine that first started in his junior year at Country Day, Williams joined the track team and allowed his humor to win over friends. Near the end of the school year, Williams's classmates voted him the "Most Humorous" student, but also the one "Least Likely to Succeed." They assumed that his tendency to fall back on humor would serve him ill in the future. This could not have been further from the truth. After graduation, Williams headed to college, his springboard to the entertainment arena.

Chapter 2

"This Kid Is Going to Make It"

$\mathbf{M}$ANY STUDENTS ENTER one college and then exit four or five years later with a degree from the same institution. That was not the case with Robin Williams. His higher education included one college, one junior college, and a famed drama institute. Together, the three educational organizations handed Williams the tools he needed to fashion an entertainment career out of the acting and comedic skills he naturally possessed.

"The Whole World Just Changed"

Williams at first had no intention of studying drama. His parents agreed to pay tuition at whatever college he wanted to attend, as long as the course of studies in which he enrolled could be used to support a career. They did not want their son to sign up for classes that would prove useless in life. They urged him to acquire knowledge he could use to embark upon a lifelong career.

Williams decided to attend Claremont Men's College, an institution thirty-five miles north of Los Angeles that emphasized programs in business and law. In the fall of 1969 he enrolled there and studied politics. He had a half-formed intention of joining the government, perhaps in the State Department where he might be sent overseas. Williams registered in a full schedule of seven classes, then almost as an afterthought added an eighth—an elective drama class in improvisation. That decision swerved him away from politics and into entertainment. Williams later said, "The whole world just changed in that one year." [22]

The improvisation class hooked Williams from its initial session. Here he could employ those talents he started exhibiting in junior high and high school, when he made students howl at his quick-flowing comments and his mimicry. Gradually, he stopped attending his other classes, which offered little that interested him anyway, and concentrated full-time on improvisation. He mentioned, "I'd go to improv class and have a blast, and I realized, 'This is exactly right. This is what I should do,' So I kept up with it."[23]

Not much mattered to Williams anymore except studying drama and improving his improvisational skills—although he did enjoy chasing girls. He had discovered how much he enjoyed dating and how much women liked being with him. His sense of humor often won them over. Away from home for the first time in his life, Williams took advantage of his freedom to see a series of girls.

When he was not dating, Williams could be found at the school's theater where he and a small group of other drama students performed as part of an improvisational group called The Synergy Trust. Williams and the others played to capacity crowds every Friday night, and through these shows Williams learned how much he loved the stage. "I'd never had so much fun in my life," he explained, "which was probably why I didn't show up for any of my other classes."[24]

Williams so rarely attended his other classes that during final examination week, one of his professors asked him who he was. Not surprisingly, Williams flunked out his freshman year, an action that forced him to face his father and make a serious choice. Unlike many parents, who might have erupted in anger, Williams's father calmly discussed the issue with his son. When Robin explained his interest in theater, his father replied that he did not mind but that he had no intention of again spending a significant sum of money to send his son away to school. Robin could look in the San Francisco area for a college, live at home, and receive instruction in drama that way. Robert Williams then advised his son to learn a backup profession, such as welding, in case an acting career failed to materialize.

A relieved Williams accepted the advice and attended a welding class. However, he did not continue studying welding for long. Williams said, "I went for one day to welding class and this man

Williams performs onstage with his trademark flamboyance. He plunged into acting as a student at Marin Junior College.

put on a mask and said, 'Basically, you can be blinded if there's an accident.' So I thought I would pass on that and keep on with the theater."[25]

He did follow his father's wishes about locating a school close by. Marin Junior College offered Williams a chance to explore his dramatic skills—and with it an opportunity for eventual stardom.

"An Incredibly Exciting Place"

Marin College in nearby Kentfield, California, offered exactly what Robin Williams sought. Under the leadership of James Dunn, the college's drama department had a national reputation for producing outstanding actors and actresses. Teachers challenged students to examine roles in different ways by staging productions

Professor James Dunn, head of Marin College's drama department, immediately recognized Williams's exceptional talent.

in unique fashion. For instance, the students might set one of English playwright William Shakespeare's dramas in the American Wild West instead of Elizabethan England. James Harper, a former student who later acted in television, said that Marin "was an incredibly exciting place with challenging theater. The teachers were incredibly exciting and they passed on that excitement to all of their students. And I think that Robin quite frankly fit in perfectly." [26]

He more than fit in—he immersed himself in the work. For the next two and one-half years, Williams studied at Marin each day, then performed at night with a San Francisco improvisational group called The Committee. He experimented with all forms of acting. He learned not only how to star in a production but how to organize and present one, and he honed his improvisation skills in front of live audiences.

His talent started to draw the attention of people. One day, he and other students rehearsed for a musical under the guidance of James Dunn, but few could seem to deliver their lines properly. As the hours dragged on, the weary students stumbled even worse, causing a few to lose their tempers. Suddenly, Williams grabbed a stick and began speaking to it in different voices, as if a crowd of fresh characters had entered the room. As a delighted Dunn watched in fascination, Williams entertained the exhausted drama students as he rapidly switched from voice to voice, a talent he would later use to humor millions. "I went home to my wife that night," mentioned Professor Dunn, "and said, 'This kid is going to make it.'" [27]

Williams backed up Dunn's prediction in 1973 when he auditioned for a scholarship to the acting program at the famous Juilliard School in New York City. Of the many students who apply to Juilliard, only the most talented are accepted. Williams faced stiff competition from at least fifty other students in the San Francisco area.

For his audition, Williams chose to perform two pieces: a speech from William Shakespeare's play *Twelfth Night* and a scene from the John Knowles novel *A Separate Peace*. The dramatic skills he had learned at Marin helped him win a coveted three-year scholarship to Juilliard. In the fall of 1973, Williams packed his bags and headed across the country to New York.

On to New York

The shock of adjusting to life in New York proved to be as awkward as his earlier introduction to California society. Williams continued to dress in bright, flowery clothes more appropriate for the beach than the big city. And he found New York residents, absorbed in the hustle and bustle of working in the nation's largest city, to be more rude than California natives.

During his first week in the city, Williams was riding a bus to school when a commuter collapsed and slumped over on the woman seated next to him. The bus driver shouted for everyone else to exit the vehicle, but Williams remained on the bus in an effort to help the stricken man. His kindness met only scorn from the bus driver, who bellowed, "He's dead, now get off! You can't do shit for him, so take your raggedy California ass and get outa my bus!" A bewildered Williams followed directions and said later, "I knew that living in New York was certainly going to be different."[28]

Other surprises awaited him when he entered Juilliard. Williams was older than the average student at the school, so administrators placed him on an advanced pace in an effort to catch him up with students who had already been at Juilliard for a few years. While this extra workload may have been disconcerting, Williams took solace in the presence of the other student placed on the same track—Christopher Reeve, who would one day play the key role in the movie *Superman*. The two became fast friends, a relationship that lasts to this day.

The exacting standards demanded by Juilliard's teachers also stretched Williams to the limit. He thought he arrived at the school well prepared to perform, but in his first week he realized how much he had to learn. Teachers told him to forget everything he had studied about acting to that date. They pointed out that he spoke too fast for a dramatic actor, that he did not project his voice to carry to the back of auditoriums, and that he mumbled too much.

Christopher Reeve recalled one of Williams's first class presentations, a skit in which Williams performed a piece from a Dudley Moore movie, *Beyond the Fringe*. The students so loved Williams's work that they applauded, something Reeve said was rarely done in class. The teacher, however, thought differently. He told Williams that instead of interpreting the character in his own manner, he had simply tried to reenact what Dudley Moore had done. He told Williams either to come back and do the piece again in his own way or forget about an acting career. The admonition rattled Williams, but it also emphasized the point that an actor had to find some way of making each role uniquely his, rather than imitating other performers.

Life at Juilliard

Williams soon fell into a rhythm at Juilliard. He avidly listened to his teachers, especially noted actor and Oscar winner John Houseman, and then tried to incorporate what he had learned into his acting. To collect spending money, Williams performed

Christopher Reeve

After graduating from Cornell University in 1974, actor Christopher Reeve studied at the Juilliard School, where he forged a lifelong friendship with Robin Williams. Reeve made his Broadway debut opposite Katharine Hepburn in *A Matter of Gravity*, which ignited a series of stage, screen, and television appearances. His most famous roles, that of the superhero in 1978's *Superman* and its subsequent sequels, and as the love-struck man in the romantic *Somewhere in Time*, established Reeve's fine reputation as an actor.

Reeve continues to work in the entertainment field despite a 1995 neck injury that left him a quadraplegic. In 1997 he directed the Emmy-nominated film *In the Gloaming*, which appeared on HBO. Reeve's 1998 autobiography, *Still Me*, spent eleven weeks on the *New York Times* best-

seller list, and in February 1999 he earned a Grammy for best spoken word album for his audio recording of the book. His most recent success occurred when he starred in a new version of the Alfred Hitchcock thriller *Rear Window*. Reeve received a nomination for a Golden Globe Award and won the Screen Actors Guild Award for best actor in a television movie or miniseries for the project.

Christopher Reeve, seen here as Superman, befriended Williams at the Juilliard School in New York City.

in whiteface as a mime at the steps of the New York Metropolitan Museum of Art. There he earned as much as $150 a day in front of large, enthusiastic crowds drawn to the scene by this unknown, talented actor.

Williams seemed to adjust to his new school, but then the holidays arrived. Since he lacked the money to return home for

Christmas, and because he was too proud to ask his father for the money, Williams remained in New York while Christopher Reeve and the other students departed. The loneliness almost overwhelmed the young man. Williams later explained in a magazine interview, "It was the first cold winter I'd experienced in many years and New York seemed unbearably bleak and lonely. One day, I started sobbing and I couldn't stop. When I ran out of tears my body just kept on going; it was like having emotional dry heaves. I went through two days like that and finally hit rock bottom and realized I had a choice; I could either tube out [crash] or level off and relax. At that point, I became like a submarine on the bottom that blows out some ballast and gets back up again."[29]

Williams illustrated the inner fortitude he exhibited in his high school freshman year, when he took matters into his own hands, lost weight, and changed the situation in which he found himself. In New York Williams faced a similar predicament, and instead of collapsing, he met the situation head-on and took control of his life. He contained his emotions, focused on his studies, and moved ahead. This would not be the last time that Williams proved he could turn his life around.

For the next two years Williams studied at Juilliard, but his unique brand of talent always seemed to perplex his teachers. They hoped to train him as they had countless other men and women, but Williams was unlike anyone they had tutored. He im-

The Juilliard School

Through the years, the Juilliard School in New York City has developed one of the finest reputations among musical and acting institutions. First founded in 1905 as the Institute of Musical Art by Dr. Frank Damrosch, the godson of famous composer Franz Liszt, the school was meant to offer a superb place of training that rivaled heralded musical academies in Europe. In 1926 the institution merged with the Juilliard Graduate School, a school funded by a significant grant from the estate of deceased wealthy textile merchant Augustus D. Juilliard. The two operated under the name the Juilliard School of Music and over the years added the famed Juilliard String Quartet and a drama division. Numerous noted actors and musicians have studied at Juilliard, including singer James Taylor, classical musician Yo-Yo Ma, and opera star Leontyne Price.

Veteran actor John Houseman taught Williams at Juilliard. Although Williams was a difficult student, Houseman acknowledged his promise as an actor.

pressed fellow students, and more than a few of his teachers, with his dramatic talents, but he always seemed to allow humor to creep in. Williams would often have the class laughing, but his instructors wanted a straight actor—no horseplay, no improvisation. "They were trying to mold Robin into a standardized Juilliard product," explained Christopher Reeve. "But Robin was too special, too original, to be that. They kept breaking him down. It's amazing how he tried [to please his teachers], how much he took."[30]

Reeve, and most of the students, responded well to the wild side in his friend. Williams's humor provided a welcome break from the long days of study. No one had seen anybody quite like Williams, a bundle of energy who never seemed to be "off." Reeve compared him to "an untied balloon that had been inflated and immediately released. I watched in awe as he virtually caromed [bounced] off the walls of the classrooms and hallways. To say that he was 'on' would be a major understatement. There was never a moment when he wasn't doing voices, imitating teachers, and making our faces ache from laughing at his antics."[31]

Even the esteemed John Houseman saw the enormous talent in the challenging student. In his dignified voice, Houseman remarked, "Mr. Williams, you are damaged but interesting."[32]

Back to California

In 1975 Williams's future took on a new path, when he met a girl back home in California with whom he fell in love. Reluctant to leave her, Williams returned to New York for his third year at Juilliard but found the separation almost unbearable. When he learned that Christopher Reeve had departed Juilliard to take an acting job in a television soap opera, Williams became even more dispirited.

The final straw occurred when his teachers, still unsure of how to handle Williams and believing he needed more training in dramatic roles, advised that he be placed back into the first year of study. This jolt, combined with the fact that the love-stricken Williams had accumulated four-hundred-dollar monthly phone bills calling his girlfriend, caused him to reject his teachers' advice, drop out of Juilliard, and head home.

He felt that he had learned enough to take a crack at San Francisco's theater community. Juilliard's intense program, even though it downplayed Williams's comedy talents, had at least instilled self-confidence in his acting abilities. Williams returned to California, intent on starting a life with his girlfriend and a career on stage as a dramatic actor. Within months, both hopes vanished, only to be replaced by better ones.

Chapter 3

"I Knew I Could Make These People Laugh"

W<small>ILLIAMS ARRIVED IN</small> San Francisco in 1975 and immediately moved in with his girlfriend. Living together proved impossible for the couple, however, and within a month or two they broke up. The ordeal devastated Williams, but he took comfort in the talent he had shown since elementary school—his humor.

"I Can Slay the Dragon There"

Williams's first wish was to act in dramatic roles, so he auditioned for parts in San Francisco theater productions. When this quickly failed because of a lack of opportunities, Williams turned to comedy. At this time comedy clubs flourished in San Francisco, and Williams found that he could both earn money and use the stage as therapy, as a way to deal with his personal problems.

His debut performance at The Intersection, a club located in the basement of an old church, produced howls of laughter and wild applause from the audience. Other comedians had failed there, but Williams won the people over with his loosely structured routine that covered a wide range of topics. Lorenzo Matawaran, a comedian who had become a regular and had seen both good and bad acts at the club, said that "Robin got up and blew everyone away,"[33] then came backstage and asked the other comedians if they thought he had been any good. Matawaran immediately noticed something special about Williams—he exuded controlled madness and frenzy onstage, as well as extreme confidence.

Within a few weeks Williams had made his mark in San Francisco comedy clubs. Besides The Intersection, he entertained at The Boarding House, The Salamander, and The Holy City Zoo, enjoying the same success no matter where he played. Audiences flocked to these clubs to catch this newcomer, who captured spectators with his sharp wit and tendency to jump from topic to topic. He explained, "I have wonderful beginnings. I'd play with them, but most of the time I couldn't find endings, so I developed a style in which I pieced things together, going from one [topic] to another with no transition." He admitted he usually had the crowds howling, but occasionally his hectic pace and far-out humor went over some people's heads. "Sometimes I'd go too far and lose people." [34]

Similar to two of his comic idols—Jonathan Winters, and star of the *Pink Panther* movies, Peter Sellers—Williams had the ability to step onstage, glance at the audience, and take off as if a giant "on" switch had been clicked. He mentioned to the *Boston Globe* that he was not sure where the material came from, but when he stepped in front of a crowd, it all just came tumbling out. He added that while his style often led to moments of joy, it also contained instances when he failed because he never knew what he might say.

Even as he became successful, Williams never outgrew the preperformance jitters. The moments before stepping onstage have often been agonizing for him. "There's total fear every time you go on," he mentioned in a magazine interview, "and it doesn't matter whether you're playing in front of twenty people or two hundred or two thousand. You get the same feeling every time, and if you don't, you're fooling yourself. Some people actually throw up before they perform." [35]

Despite these fears, Williams discovered that performing helped him deal with painful issues in his own life. Williams could go before people in a comedy club and say things he would never mention one-on-one and, in doing so, purge whatever mental demons might be afflicting him. He admits that he has difficulty talking to one or two people in social gatherings, but place him before two thousand spectators and a spark ignites. "Performing is a different world," he said. "It's total freedom, it's mine, my world. I can slay the dragon there." [36]

Williams claims that when he is onstage, he feels as if he has a license to be crazy that people in normal situations would never

Jonathan Winters

Jonathan Winters, Robin Williams's comic idol, was born in Dayton, Ohio, on November 11, 1925. After serving two and a half years with the marines in the South Pacific during World War II, he returned to Ohio and attended college. From there he headed to the Dayton Art Institute. At his wife's urging, in 1946 Winters entered a local talent contest in Dayton. His performance helped him win a job as an early morning disc jockey on a local radio station in Dayton.

In 1953, Winters used his family's meager savings to move to New York. His work in nightclubs there soon attracted huge audiences. He made television appearances on different programs, such as *The Jack Paar Show*, *The Steve Allen Show*, and *The Tonight Show*, and proved he belonged with the esteemed names in comedy.

Noted for his unique rapid-paced style of humor, Winters drew packed crowds who loved watching him turn a simple prop or word into a protracted routine. Robin Williams avidly followed Winters's skits and credited the man with influencing his career.

Jonathan Winters inspired and influenced Williams's comic style.

have. He can act out his fantasies, explore and resolve painful situations, and fashion worlds in his own image. Instead of paying a psychiatrist for therapy, Williams faced his demons onstage. As one friend explained of Williams's frantic performances, "You know, he has to do it." [37]

South to Hollywood

In between comedy acts, Williams briefly tended bar. One night in early 1976 an attractive twenty-six-year-old dancer and graduate student named Valerie Velardi walked into the club where he worked, sat down, and started watching the bartender instead of the comedian on stage. Not only was the bartender handsome, but he seemed to create new characters and facial features to serve each customer. Williams also noticed her. Soon the pair started dating, and within a month he and Velardi had moved in together. "Was it love at first sight?" commented Williams. "More like lust."[38]

Velardi gave Williams more than companionship. Two years older than the comedian, she offered a maturity the younger man lacked. She began keeping notes on his routines and organizing them into files of material on similar topics. Williams had always kept his material in his head. But thanks to Velardi's system, he gained a steadily growing library of material from which he could fashion new routines and improve old ones.

Williams's first wife, Valerie Velardi, helped him develop his comedy act and encouraged him to move to Los Angeles.

As Williams became more popular in San Francisco, he faced a crucial decision. He could either remain in the city and maintain his moderate success, or he could head to the entertainment center—Los Angeles—to see if he could succeed in the rigorous comedy market that existed there. Every comedian who wanted to become famous knew that to be considered a star, one had to make it in Los Angeles. As a result, the city flourished with comedians competing with each other. The city could make a star of Robin Williams or relegate him to the backwaters of entertainment.

Though Velardi had her own dreams of a dancing career, she urged Williams to leave San Francisco and move to Los Angeles. Only then would he know how good he could be. Williams hesitated. He had started to carve out a decent living in San Francisco, but he knew Velardi was correct. He said, "I always wanted to hit it big, but I thought it would be easier in San Francisco, where there was less competition. It was Val who made the sacrifice. She dropped her own career to help me with mine. She encouraged me, almost ordered me, to go to Hollywood."[39]

In late 1976 Williams and Velardi headed south to Los Angeles. They moved into a modest-looking neighborhood, unpacked their belongings and a pet parrot named Cora whom Robin trained to say "Birds can't talk,"[40] and set out to conquer the comedy world.

"The Funniest Guy I've Ever Seen"

Robin Williams wasted little time carving out a niche in the comedy realm. Soon after arriving in Los Angeles, he headed to The Comedy Store, a famous nightclub frequented by notable comics and up-and-coming hopefuls. Each night the club hosted an open microphone segment, during which unknown comedians received the opportunity to perform in front of the enthusiastic, yet critical, crowds. Most of these audiences also included agents, producers, or directors seeking the next big talent. At The Comedy Store, men and women, with dreams of fame, either rocketed their careers to a fast start with a rousing rendition or left the stage humiliated with the sound of catcalls and derision ringing in their

The Comedy Store

Los Angeles's renowned nightclub The Comedy Store opened in 1972 on Sunset Boulevard and helped start long careers for many comedians besides Robin Williams. Some of the club's many distinguished alumni include Jim Carrey, David Letterman, Paul Rodriguez, Garry Shandling, Arsenio Hall, Gallagher, Howie Mandel, Jackie Mason, Craig T. Nelson, Chris Tucker, George Carlin, Damon Wayans, Pauly Shore, Sandra Bernhard, Whoopi Goldberg, Roseanne, Richard Pryor, and Eddie Murphy.

ears. Williams, who watched many comedians fail miserably on that stage, compared the ordeal to what the gladiators faced in the ancient Roman arena.

Before he stepped onstage for the first time, nerves so rattled Williams that he feared he would become ill. All it took, though, were a few lines from his outlandish mind, and the crowd was his. "My stomach was in my shoes, I was so scared," he recalled. "But after less than a minute I felt comfortable. I knew I could make these people laugh."[41] The audience howled at the fresh comic's strange, almost twisted, way of looking at things and loved the vast cast of characters that populated the act. Williams scored such a resounding triumph that the owners of The Comedy Store immediately signed him to a regular contract paying two hundred dollars per week. The comedian had taken a huge first step.

Williams quickly became a regular at the top Los Angeles comedy clubs, including The Improv and other popular establishments. He also joined a group of aspiring comedians and actors studying at the Harvey Lembeck Comedy Workshop under the prominent performer Harvey Lembeck. Lembeck shouted topics to the comics, who then had to quickly present a routine based on the idea. Not surprisingly, Williams excelled at this improvisational challenge and quickly outpaced his fellow students. Lembeck remembered one time when he asked the group to pretend they were telephoning someone to explain why they were late for an appointment. The other comedians telephoned doctors or lawyers, but when Robin Williams's turn arrived, he created a scene in which he called God.

Fellow student John Ritter, who later starred in the popular 1970s situation comedy *Three's Company*, initially dismissed the shabbily dressed Williams but quickly changed his mind when he saw him perform. Ritter said, "I saw the way this dude was dressed in baggy pants, suspenders, a beaten-up tux over high-topped sneakers, a straw hat with the brim falling off, John Lennon glasses with no glass in the frames, and I thought, 'Well, this guy is definitely going for the sight gag.' I was almost a bit suspicious. So I watched carefully, and he turned out to be the funniest guy I've ever seen."[42]

"How Are You Going to Top the Original?"

During one of Williams's performances at The Comedy Store in 1977, George Schlatter sat in the audience and scrutinized every

Williams strikes a whimsical pose in front of The Comedy Store. His success at the Los Angeles comedy club led to television opportunities.

word. Schlatter had become a well-known Hollywood producer, mainly on the success of a television program called *Laugh-In*. The outrageous 1960s comedy show was the precursor to *Saturday Night Live*. Schlatter was in the process of assembling the cast for a new version of *Laugh-In* and had been scouting local comedy clubs in hopes of catching fresh talent. He visited The Comedy Store after hearing of a new entertainer named Robin Williams who delighted audiences each week.

Schlatter, who had worked with the top performers in Hollywood and thus was a difficult man to impress, instantly warmed to Williams. He was not thrilled about the performer's

Producer George Schlatter discovered Williams at The Comedy Store and cast him in the TV program Laugh-In.

appearance. The barefooted Williams sported a full beard and shoulder-length hair and wore coveralls and a cowboy hat. But he loved Williams's wide-ranging routines. After the show, Schlatter offered Williams a contract that paid a then-princely salary of fifteen hundred dollars a week. He had one condition— Williams had to cut his hair, shave his beard, and dress more suitably. The comedian, who thought he had hit the jackpot, readily agreed.

Unfortunately, the new show did not enjoy the same success as the groundbreaking *Laugh-In*. After fourteen weeks, network executives canceled the program, and Williams found himself looking for a new job. Within a span of three months, the comedian had soared to what he thought was the pinnacle of comedy success and then plummeted. "Unfortunately, doing a remake of a show which had been one of the milestones of TV was a little like doing *Jaws VI*," explained Williams, referring to the difficulty in duplicating a masterpiece. "How are you going to top the original?"[43]

In addition, the show never allowed Williams to employ his wit and improvisational skills. Instead, the show's creators asked him to stick closely to the script. Williams did, but the move failed because it did not allow the comic to express the very talent the producers had hired him for.

Despite the failure, *Laugh-In* exposed Williams to a larger audience than he could ever enjoy in a comedy club. His name became more recognizable in Hollywood, and he met noted individuals who walked away impressed with what they had seen. Actress Bette Davis, a guest on the show, immediately recognized Williams's talent. She believed that the young comedian would eventually attain immense success, and she warned him that one day his biggest problem would be learning how to say no to the countless number of producers, directors, and friends who would implore him to do them a favor or appear in their show.

An Agent and a Wife

On the strength of his *Laugh-In* performances, Williams landed parts in other television shows. He joined the cast of *The Richard*

Comedian Richard Pryor was one of Williams's idols. After his stint on Laugh-In, *Williams joined the cast of* The Richard Pryor Show.

Pryor Show, a program hosted by one of his comic idols, Richard Pryor, who had risen to fame on the basis of daring, often obscene, humor. Williams also had brief appearances in *Fernwood 2 Night,* an early satire of late-night shows hosted by comedian Martin Mull.

Williams could also always count on his stand-up act to make a living. As long as the comedy nightclubs thrived, he could survive, and the chance always existed that some other prominent individual would walk in and offer him a contract.

In the spring of 1978, Williams got another chance. Larry Brezner, a man who represented many performers for a major talent agency, watched Williams work with Harvey Lembeck's group. Brezner loved how quickly a fresh routine would materialize out of the comedian's mind, as if he had already known what concepts would be tossed to him by Lembeck. "I saw energy coming out of this person onstage that was shocking," said Brezner. "Afterward, as soon as I could get him to slow down enough, we talked for five minutes. He told me he did standup, and I began following him around."[44] Brezner signed on as Williams's agent and began contacting everyone he knew in Hollywood.

With an agent promising bigger and better things for him, Williams took another leap on June 4, 1978, and married Valerie Velardi. Everything now appeared to be in place—a solid beginning in entertainment, a supportive wife, and a powerful agent. Before the year ended, Williams introduced a new character to television. It was a unique role that vaulted him to wealth and acclaim.

Chapter 4

"I Am Mork from Ork"

SURPRISINGLY, ROBIN WILLIAMS'S agent was not the catalyst for his first huge break. Brezner brought studio executives to The Comedy Store to catch the comedian in person, but Williams proved to be a little too wild for some. A group of United Artist executives, for instance, walked out in the middle of the show, claiming Williams was crazy and stating he would never make it in television or film. Meanwhile, though, the grade school son of a Hollywood producer made a suggestion to his father that led to the creation of Mork from Ork—and instant celebrity for Williams.

"The Only Martian Who Applied"

In 1977 producer/director Garry Marshall had one of television's hottest programs in *Happy Days*. Starring Ron Howard and Henry Winkler, the comedy series focused on the antics of a group of high school students living in the United States during the 1950s.

One day Marshall's son, Scott, told his father that he should put an alien into the series. Marshall, who knew a good idea when he heard one, thought this could work as a one-time guest appearance. After all, the nation lived through an alien craze in the 1950s, so the premise was not implausible. He asked his writers to craft a script in which an alien visited Earth to study the people.

Marshall at first turned to one of Williams's comic role models, Jonathan Winters, as his choice to play Mork, but the entertainer declined the offer. When Marshall's second choice, Dom DeLuise, also opted out, Marshall announced open auditions for the role.

Close to fifty actors appeared for the audition, but most failed to meet expectations. Robin Williams changed that. One of the show's producers, Jerry Paris, explained that after a long day of watching auditions, many of them painfully miserable, Williams walked in near the end of the audition. Paris instantly noticed something different about this actor. He said, "They [the previous acts] were all terrible. About five o'clock in walked this boy with rainbow suspenders. When he sat down, I asked if he could sit a little differently, the way an alien might. Immediately he sat on his head. We hired him."[45]

Williams later admitted that he purposely made outrageous noises and gestures in hopes of distancing himself from the other actors and landing the role. His tactics worked, as no one came close to making the impact on the producers that Williams had. Referring to the comedian's outrageousness, Garry Marshall stated, with a mixture of humor and truth, that Williams landed the part because "he was the only Martian who applied."[46]

Few viewers had seen anything like the whirlwind that buzzed into *Happy Days*. During his episode, Williams let loose with a barrage of bizarre movements and hilarious lines, similar to what he had become known for in his nightclub acts. The show became one of *Happy Days'* most popular segments and produced an avalanche of mail to the network, the American Broadcasting Company (ABC). The appearance of Mork received more fan mail

Happy Days

The television show that introduced Mork to the world had its own successful run. After *Happy Days'* debut on January 15, 1974, the show steadily rose in the ratings and lasted until 1984.

Set in the 1950s in Milwaukee, Wisconsin, *Happy Days* told the story of the Cunningham family through the eyes of the main character, a teenager named Richie Cunningham, played by Ron Howard. Each episode placed Cunningham and his high school friends in a different predicament. These problems were sometimes solved by the most famous character of the cast, the Fonz, played by Henry Winkler. In 1980 the Smithsonian Museum of American History, in Washington, D.C., recognized *Happy Days'* value to entertainment when it honored the series by putting one of the Fonz's leather jackets on display.

Williams appears as Mork from Ork on Happy Days. *The alien was so popular that network executives created a TV show centered around the character.*

than any other episode. Overwhelmed by the public's response, network executives decided to place Mork in his own series.

At first the network executives planned to place the new show into one of its lesser-appealing time slots, against a rival network's popular show. However, when they read the drafts of the first few shows and saw how delightfully unique this new character was, they quickly placed the show into one of its choicest places—its then-popular Thursday night lineup. Mork, and with him Robin Williams, was about to grab the nation's attention.

"Wow, They Noticed Me"

The first episode of the new series, titled *Mork and Mindy,* aired September 14, 1978. Robin Williams, playing Mork from Ork, is dispatched to Earth from his planet as punishment for constantly making fun of Ork's leader, Orson. Mork is given the task of observing earthlings and reporting what he has gathered each week to Orson.

Mork arrives in the Rocky Mountains near Boulder, Colorado, in a giant eggshell (a standard method of transportation on Ork), dons a suit that conforms to those worn on Earth, and starts to trek around the area. What Mork does not know is that he has put the suit on backward. He eventually meets Mindy, a clerk in a music store played by actress Pam Dawber, who agrees to take him in and introduce him to Earth habits.

When neighbors become suspicious of this strange newcomer, a competency hearing is held in court to determine if Mork is sane enough to care for himself. Mork prepares for the courtroom hearing by watching reruns of famed courtroom television shows, such as *Perry Mason,* and the movie *Inherit the Wind.* He convinces the judge that he is harmless, and Mork and Mindy return home. As was true of every segment, the show ends with Mork giving a report to Orson—a clever tactic that allowed Mork to comment on some human foible, injustice, or oddity.

Like the appearance in *Happy Days,* Williams's performance instantly captivated the nation. Viewers warmed to the unusual combination of Mork's childlike manner of observing humans while appearing to be an adult. He looked old enough to be a father or an older brother, yet he exuded the youthful enthusiasm and delightful honesty exhibited by children. That is what made it so difficult for Mindy to explain complicated human actions and emotions such as bigotry and war to Mork—she had to relate everything as if talking to an eight-year-old child. For the first time, but not the last, Williams earned recognition playing a man-child.

Viewers went crazy over the new show. Stores had trouble keeping rainbow suspenders—which Williams incorporated into the Mork character—in stock, and school kids ran around playgrounds shouting Mork's catchphrase, "Nanu, nanu."

Fame came suddenly to Robin Williams. After the first episode of *Mork and Mindy,* he and his wife went to dinner with some friends, including Bennett Tramer, who later produced the successful television program, *Saved by the Bell.* Tramer said later, "Some kid saw him and said, 'You look like Mork from Ork.' Robin said, 'I am Mork from Ork.' There was something sweet about his reaction. Sort of, 'Wow, they noticed me.' Two weeks after that he couldn't go to a mall without being mobbed." [47]

Within two weeks the show soared into television's top ten, then finished its first season at number three. More than 60 million people watched Williams every week to see what new predicament Mork confronted, and Williams became an inspiration to the hopeful comedians who dreamed of hitting it big. In two years, he had gone from playing local comedy clubs to starring in a hit television show.

Pam Dawber smiles at Williams's antics in a scene from Mork and Mindy. *The show was an instant hit and brought Williams celebrity status.*

Barely Controlled Frenzy

When he steps onstage, Robin Williams allows all the creative juices to gush out. He holds nothing back as he covers a broad range of topics and utilizes numerous voices and characterizations. At times, members of the audience wonder where he gets his unique material. Williams explained to writer John Eskow of *Rolling Stone* magazine in a 1979 interview, "Sometimes it gets a little scary [onstage]. Like one night my wife, Valerie, said, 'Ooooh, that was like a little breakdown there!' It can be very intense. When you're really out there, releasing the tension and generating energy, it's like a sponge bath, a whole cleaning process."

"Our Kitchen's All Screwed up Because of You"

One of the reasons for *Mork and Mindy*'s success was that the producers and directors allowed Williams to employ the talent that had made him successful—his improvisational skills. Williams was not able to freewheel every word and line, but the writers handed him a script, then gave him freedom within that structure to veer into material that only he could create. A story line had to be followed, but no one on the set, sometimes not even Williams, knew what he might do to the story or how he might react to the other performers. Viewers tuned in to the weekly show anticipating that Williams, as Mork, would suddenly launch into a hilarious routine. And the writers often expected Williams to use some of the material he had incorporated into his stand-up performances.

Williams enjoyed the unusual freedom handed him. He said, "I wasn't restrained at all, because they basically took what I did [in his comedy club appearances] and put it into TV. They would take whole sections of my act and write episodes around them."[48]

The actors and actresses surrounding Williams on the show were selected for their ability to smoothly react to whatever Williams tossed at them. They also realized who possessed the major star presence. One director who worked on the series said, "Everybody here is aware that this is really 'The Robin Williams Show.' My job is to make sure Robin doesn't go so far off the wall that only seven people in the audience understand what he's doing."[49]

Occasionally, Williams encountered difficulties with the network censors, whose job it was to ensure nothing controversial or

Jonathan Winters (in crib) and Pam Dawber act alongside Williams in an episode of Mork and Mindy. *The producers of the show allowed Williams to improvise material.*

indecent crept in and shattered the program's wholesomeness. Williams loved to see how far he could go on certain subjects to test the censors, but he rarely pushed the limits to such an extreme that producers had to rein him in.

The show was unique, in part, because the program's humor appealed to people of different age levels—both adults and children enjoyed watching. Younger viewers loved Mork's handful of Orkian slogans, his flat-footed, childlike gait, and his clothes, including his rainbow suspenders, while adults became enamored with Mork's ability to cut through hypocrisy and see the earth though youthful eyes. Mork's amazement at learning things for the first time reminded parents of their own children's early discoveries of nature and the world. Williams, relying on his experience as a New York mime, conveyed these messages with a potent mixture of words and gestures. "There were enough adult references," explained Williams, "and the children loved the innocence of it. I would have kids come up and throw an egg in the air and shout 'Fly' [a reference to Orkians being born in eggshells] and you could hear their parents go, 'Our kitchen's all screwed up because of you.'" [50]

"Inspiration Is Like Drilling for Oil"

Robin Williams's work on the television series did not take him from his comedy club performances. On weekends and often at night after working on the television set, Williams headed to one or more of his favorite spots to try out new material and to interact with live audiences. He feared that if he abandoned the nightclubs, his roots, he might lose touch not only with his audiences but also with his ability to recognize what worked and what did not.

Williams constantly tried to concoct new material, some of which he quickly discarded after realizing it would not work with audiences. He understood, though, that if he kept his mind churning, sooner or later he would produce usable routines. "Inspiration is like drilling for oil," he said. "Sometimes I can think for hours and come up with nothing, and then in a few minutes it all comes in waves. Maybe you have to go through those hours of dead time, like a drill bit piercing the shale and the old sediment, to get to it, the new stuff."[51]

Based upon his newfound popularity, the comedian branched into different areas. He acted as a frequent host or visitor to the groundbreaking late night show *Saturday Night Live,* and he cut his first album based on his stand-up material. Titled *Reality . . . What a Concept,* the album sold more than 1 million copies, won a 1979 Grammy for best comedy album, and further added to Williams's reputation.

Other honors besides the Grammy poured in for Williams. He received a 1978 Emmy Award nomination for outstanding lead actor in a comedy series, a Golden Apple Award bestowed by the Hollywood Women's Press Club for his work on *Mork and Mindy,*

"A Sensitive Guy"

Like many performers, Robin Williams has a vulnerable, sensitive side. In 1982 writer Lawrence Linderman visited Williams at his ranch to do an interview for *Playboy* magazine. When he arrived, Williams was watching the movie, *On the Waterfront,* a film containing a powerful ending in which the main character receives a severe beating. During those final moments, Linderman looked over at Williams and saw tears pouring down his cheeks. Linderman later added, "I don't think I've ever interviewed a more sensitive guy. Or a gentler one, for that matter."

and a 1979 Golden Globe Award for best actor in a television comedy series. His new fame enabled Williams to purchase a gorgeous home in luxurious Topanga Canyon north of Los Angeles. He also maintained apartments in Hollywood and San Francisco and a ranch in the Napa Valley.

The Troubles of Fame

With fame, however, came trouble. Other comedians accused Williams of stealing some of their material. Williams responded by admitting that at times he might have used similar lines, but claimed that it was the result of visiting so many nightclubs and hearing so much material. In fact, he said, he and the other comics often traded lines back and forth until no one actually knew who originated what material. In the end, no comedian threatened a lawsuit or accused Williams of being unfair. They understood that if he repeated any of their lines, he did so unintentionally. Also, whenever Williams discovered that he used another comic's lines, which was not often, he made a habit of quickly paying the individual.

Williams also had difficulty turning down the numerous requests that flooded in. Friends deluged his office asking that he appear at their charity events or that he open a new club. Combined with his work on the series and his love of performing many nights at comedy clubs, Williams enjoyed little time to himself. Bette Davis's belief that Williams would have trouble saying no to people materialized just as she had expected.

Williams explained why he had such trouble saying no in an episode of *Mork and Mindy.* In the segment, Robin Williams as himself visits Boulder, Colorado, and meets with Mork and Mindy. When Mindy asked Robin Williams what the biggest drawback to fame was, he answered, "I guess I felt really afraid to say no to them [friends] because then they'd all say, 'Oh, Robin Williams. Mr. Smarty Pants. Big shot. You forgot your old friends. You can't lend me ten thousand dollars for a new car. You won't do the Save the Shrimp benefit.'" [52]

Those problems compounded when Williams entered a new phase of his career. As happens to many television stars, Hollywood hoped to capitalize on his popularity by placing him in his own film. But Williams encountered a rough road on this new trail.

Williams rests during a celebrity tennis match. As his fame grew, Williams was asked to appear at charity events and other functions.

"Oh God, When Is This Going to Be Over?"

Williams's film career actually started before his work in *Mork and Mindy*. In 1977 he acted in scenes for a movie called *Can I Do It . . . Till I Need Glasses?*, an undistinguished comedy. The director cut Williams's scenes before releasing the movie, but reedited the film and added Williams's work after the success of *Mork and Mindy*. The comedian prefers to forget the movie and instead points to another film as the beginning of his Hollywood career.

In 1978 Christopher Reeve, Williams's old friend from Juilliard, starred in the title role of the blockbuster film *Superman*. Since transforming that comic book hero into a movie proved successful, Hollywood producers searched for similar vehicles that might be profitable. Director Richard Altman thought he found one in the longtime comic strip character, Popeye. When Williams won the role as Popeye in 1980, he thought he had his ticket to movie stardom.

Williams immediately discovered that this dream was not meant to be. Numerous production difficulties, special effects failures, miserable weather, and a mundane script doomed the project. "After the first day [of shooting] on *Popeye* I thought, 'Well, maybe this isn't it,' and I finally wound up going, 'Oh God, when is this going to be over?'" [53]

The process dragged on for months. Robert Altman refused to let Williams improvise. Budgeting problems forced the pro-

Williams plays the title character in Robert Altman's 1980 film, Popeye. *The film faced a number of problems during shooting and it flopped in theaters.*

ducers to cut back in certain areas, especially special effects, so Williams labored every day in awkward, ill-fitting fake rubber arms that made him look bloated instead of muscular. Finally, the mumbling, raspy voice Williams used to imitate Popeye was difficult for audiences to understand.

By the time the movie's climactic final scene was to be shot, the exasperated crew was ready to hurry through it and get home. But Williams, who had almost given up on the movie's chances, knew that the last opportunity to rescue the film lay in fashioning an attention-grabbing ending. He recalled,

> On the last day of shooting, we were struggling desperately to come up with an ending, and we all knew it would take great special effects to pull it off. I'd pictured Popeye flying through the air, sort of like the cartoon thing in which he becomes a tornado with his legs spinning around at warp speed. And I know that I was supposed to punch an octopus out of the water and have it go whirring into space, but that didn't happen, either.[54]

What viewers received instead was a mechanical octopus with limp arms that posed little threat to Popeye. Williams, relieved to be finished, headed home with the slim hope that audiences would, at least, be kind.

They were not. A Hollywood premier audience, with Williams in agonizing attendance, sat in embarrassed silence as the movie unfolded, and critics lambasted the product. Ticket purchasers hoped to experience Robin Williams as Mork, or as the nightclub comedian, but instead they received a rubbery caricature that connected with no one.

Cancellation of a Series

Williams's troubles with Popeye could be dismissed as a one-time occurrence, since he still had a hit television show. However, that started to change in the series' second season. In an attempt to wrest a Sunday night audience from a rival network, ABC shifted the show from its popular Thursday time slot to Sunday. This pitted *Mork and Mindy* against the ratings powerhouse *Archie Bunker's Place,* a program featuring one of television's most popular characters,

Useful Comedy

Robin Williams first learned that his series *Mork and Mindy* had been canceled by reading about it in the newspapers while on the set of a children's special. Instead of sulking, however, he let comedy brighten the moment. Comedian Eric Idle, also present at the time, explained Williams's reaction in a quote appearing in Andy Dougan's book *Robin Williams*.

> The end of the show wasn't unexpected, but you don't think you'll find out by having someone hand you a newspaper when you're on a set. Robin gathered the technicians around him and did a routine about TV executives. Everyone was on the floor [laughing] and it was behind him. I thought that was the most useful example of comedy that I'd ever seen.

Archie Bunker. Instead of maintaining its audience, *Mork and Mindy* plummeted in the ratings and failed to reach the top twenty shows.

As the ratings plunged, the network made more mistakes and lost more viewers. Forgetting that Mork's appeal rested, in part, on his childlike innocence, the network instead ordered the show's writers to place Mork in outrageous situations, such as trying to join a pro football cheerleading squad or battling aliens headed by bombshell actress Raquel Welch and a *Playboy* playmate. More viewers abandoned the show when a weirder character than Mork, Exidor, joined the cast. Exidor's strange reactions and emotional eruptions distracted the show's audience. The public had responded to Mork's interactions with average humans, not his antics with a crazed individual. Once the producers abandoned the childlike Mork, the series lost its impact.

Williams had decided to leave the show after its third season, but producers enticed him to remain by adding a new character—Jonathan Winters. Williams could not pass up the opportunity to play alongside his longtime hero, so he agreed to another year.

That season ended unsuccessfully as well. Mork and Mindy fell in love, married, and gave birth to a child, played by Winters. (On Ork, people are born old and then grow younger.) The ploy, however, failed to gain viewers, and near the end of the season ABC canceled the show. The final program aired on June 10, 1982.

Williams now had two recent failures with which to contend—*Popeye* and the cancellation of his show. He stood at a crossroads in his career, and the path he first selected led to pain and personal tragedy.

Chapter 5

The Deadly Sins of Hollywood Wait for Everyone

FOLLOWING THE DEMISE of his television show, Williams concentrated on making movies. Hollywood still considered him a hot commodity and thought that he could star in profitable projects. The first five films he made after *Popeye* failed to meet expectations, but others were well received. At the same time, personal problems troubled the young comedian.

"From Marvel Comics to Tolstoy"

Williams enjoyed more success with his next film, *The World According to Garp*. The director, George Roy Hill, believed that Williams could perform in a dramatic role if given the chance and the proper direction. Whereas most people judged Williams to be a comedian trying to act in serious drama, Hill considered him an actor who also excelled at comedy.

Williams warmed to Hill's careful handling. In one of their first meetings, Hill let Williams know that, instead of varying from the script, he wanted the actor to focus on the character as he was written and try to understand what made him do the things he did. This forced Williams to abandon his usual tendency to consider the script as little more than a loose structure that could easily be altered. It also made him examine human emotions and motives.

The experience helped to challenge Williams as an actor. He explained, "It was like going from Marvel Comics to Tolstoy [noted

Russian author]. The hero, T.S. Garp, is like another side of me, the nonperforming side. It was a process for me of mentally stripping away, getting back to what I was doing when I was an acting student at Juilliard."[55] He loved the chance of returning to what he considered his acting roots, his education as a dramatic actor.

"It's Hard to Find Movies I Want to Do"

The movie fared decently at the box office and critics praised Williams's acting, but the public still expected to see a comedy when they attended a Robin Williams movie. That was made obvious by the results of his next two projects, both dramas. In 1983 *The Survivors* flopped at the box office. The next year *Moscow on the Hudson* strengthened Williams's claim as a straight actor but failed to earn significant money. "The good news about *Moscow on the Hudson*," wrote *Newsweek* magazine, "is the surprising ease with which Robin Williams enters the skin of this confused, ambitious, melancholy Russian. His sweet, touching performance makes one forget Williams the manic comedian."[56]

Despite this and other positive reviews, Williams failed to register a victory where he needed it most—at the box office. This continued with his next two films, even though both were comedies. *The Best of Times* was about a former high school football player who wants to relive a crucial football game. And *Club*

The Honesty of Children

Making movies can be a double-edged sword, as Robin Williams has found when it comes to his children. On the one hand, he can use film to entertain and delight them. He took many roles because he felt his children would like them. He said in Andy Dougan's book, *Robin Williams*, "My kids don't analyze what I do. They just have a natural reaction to a film and they laugh if they think it's funny."

On the other hand, his children can sometimes toss a movie back in their father's face, showing they do analyze some things. Stephen J. Spignesi quotes Williams as saying that he sometimes has a tough time using himself as an example to his kids because he made movies that bombed. If he tried to correct his children or point out a mistake they made, they sometimes responded, "Hey, you made *Toys* [a movie that fared dismally at the box office]."

Eddie Murphy performs a stand-up set. Murphy and other famous comedians landed the film roles that Williams wanted.

Paradise told the story of a retired fireman who heads to the Caribbean. Neither film made much money, and both garnered little acclaim for Williams. He now had the distinction of making nine films that failed to earn significant returns for investors.

Williams's reputation in Hollywood plummeted as a result. A California magazine that year compiled a list of what was "In" and "Out" and stated that attending any party at which Robin Williams appeared was now "Out." Producers pondered whether Williams might be a one-show wonder and feared that *Mork and Mindy* might have been his only claim to stardom. Quality roles stopped being offered to him. "It's hard to find movies I want to do," he said at the time. "I'm usually third string behind [comedians] Eddie [Murphy], Bill [Murray] or Steve [Martin]—and sometimes Chevy [Chase]." [57]

Lawsuit Problems

Being a famous comedian brings numerous benefits, but it also delivers its share of difficulties. On April 26, 1988, Williams became entangled in a messy lawsuit when a former girlfriend, Tish Carter, filed suit claiming that Williams infected her with a disease that caused great emotional pain. Williams denied any wrongdoing and wanted to answer the charges immediately, but his lawyers advised him to remain silent while the matter worked its way through the court. Williams's attorneys filed a countersuit stating Carter resorted to the legal system only by suing to make money off the famous entertainer. Six days before the case was to go to trial, the two sides reached an agreement that settled the dispute.

Swimming with Small Sharks

At the same time that his movie career stalled, Williams's fast-paced lifestyle added more problems. He had developed a habit of partying excessively. He sometimes attended as many as five parties in one night, where he joked, visited, and often shared drugs until the early hours of the morning. "There was always someone somewhere to keep partying with," he explained. "Hollywood is designed that way. And the temptations are so many and varied. There is everything. The deadly sins of Hollywood. They wait for everyone."[58]

This heavy involvement in the nightlife hampered Williams as a performer. He later admitted that he lost his focus and stopped creating imaginative routines.

The more deeply Williams sank into the drug world, the less creative he became. Like many people involved with cocaine, alcohol, and other drugs, Williams believed he could handle it, a notion he discarded when he finally attained sobriety. He observed, "To say that you do just a little cocaine is like saying you're swimming with just a small shark."[59]

Along with drugs and fame came attention from women, who were drawn to movie and television stars. Williams found the attention too enticing to ignore, and he had a series of brief affairs. Not surprisingly, this caused problems at home, where he and Velardi fought frequently. All this, combined with drug use, distracted Williams from his acting and comedy.

The Death of John Belushi

However, two events in the early 1980s stunned Williams into sobriety. The first was the death of a close friend. On March 5, 1982, Williams visited a comedy club, where a bouncer informed him that actor Robert De Niro and comedian John Belushi, a star performer on *Saturday Night Live*, wanted to see him.

Williams drove to Belushi's apartment, where he was astounded to see half-empty wine bottles and trash littering the room. What most shocked him, however, was his friend's condition— Belushi looked dazed and barely in control. De Niro was not present, but Williams spotted a rough-looking woman sharing cocaine with Belushi. Belushi's head suddenly dropped and then, about five seconds later, the comedian looked up.

Comedian John Belushi died of a drug overdose in 1982. His death prompted Williams to stop drinking and doing drugs.

Williams asked his friend if he was all right. Belushi replied that, even though he had taken cocaine and other drugs, he was all right. Williams shared some cocaine with Belushi and then, feeling uncomfortable, left after spending only ten minutes with the comedian. When he arrived home, he told Valerie about his encounter with Belushi and added, "God, man, he was with this lady—she was tough, scary." [60] Williams was concerned for his friend.

The next day, Pam Dawber informed Williams that Belushi had died the night before of a drug overdose. At a loss for words, Williams finally muttered that he had been there. All day, Williams thought about the incident and worried about the similarities between Belushi's and his life. Belushi was about the same age as Williams, and the two had comparable lifestyles. When Williams noticed a concerned Dawber staring at him, he reassured her with words that have emerged from many drug users' mouths, some who successfully follow through and others who do not, "Don't you worry, Dawbs. It'll never happen to me." [61]

Though Williams played no role in Belushi's death, in the tragedy's aftermath he felt guilty. He wondered if he should have known what would happen and if he might have been able to help his friend. Most of all, though, the incident terrified him, for he saw in Belushi a mirror image of himself—young, popular, funny, seemingly indestructible, and now dead. He and Belushi ran in the same circles and lived the same high-paced lifestyle.

Those thoughts frightened Robin Williams. He told a television interviewer how the episode affected him:

> Here's a guy who was probably one of the toughest, strongest people you could ever meet—and he's taken out. Basically, it cleaned up a whole generation of people because this guy was as strong as anybody you could ever meet. I mean, a *bull.* John, for a laugh, could run into that wall. And get up and do it again. So if it took him out, you realize that we're all pretty mortal. [62]

Williams adopted a healthier routine after Belushi's death. He gradually removed drugs and alcohol from his life, and he made sure to keep in better shape. To distance himself from the drug

A tough cop.

Williams and his son Zachary arrive at a New York movie premiere in 2002. Williams's desire to be a good father encouraged him to get sober.

scene, he and Valerie spent much more time on their ranch near San Francisco than in Hollywood.

"Just Be Daddy"

The second event that ripped Williams out of the drug scene was the birth of his son Zachary in April 1983. He wanted to be there for his child, to enjoy watching him grow and experience new things. Williams feared he would miss all that if he continued to use cocaine and alcohol.

As Zach grew older, the father and son loved to watch old Warner Brothers cartoons on television. During the shows Williams tossed in his own remarks in funny voices as interaction with the cartoon characters. Sometimes this amused the son; other times it did not. Williams remembered, "Sometimes while the cartoons are showing I do wacky voices—you know, the way I do in my act. Sometimes he likes that, but sometimes he says, 'Daddy, don't use that voice. Just be Daddy.'"[63]

"She's Robin's Anchor"

One change Williams failed to implement, however, involved women—he still conducted frequent affairs. He and Valerie engaged in such heated arguments about the affairs that Zach burst out in temper tantrums. In an effort to bring some stability into the child's life, the couple hired a nanny named Marsha Garces in 1984. Garces moved out to the Williamses' Napa Valley ranch to live full-time with the boy. Garces had an immediate calming effect on Zach, and subsequently the tantrums dwindled.

Unfortunately, the strife between Robin and Valerie failed to abate. They rarely appeared in public together, and when Robin learned that his wife had begun to see another man, he exploded in anger. Marsha Garces, who had also become Williams's personal assistant, bluntly told him that he had little right to be angry at his wife for doing what he had been doing to her for years.

More and more, Marsha Garces brought direction and confidence to Williams's life. She reminded him that he was a decent man and that he had plenty of talent, but that he had wasted much of it by living recklessly. When she casually remarked one day that if the comedian were not so messed up, she might be interested in him, Williams began to look at her in a romantic way. By late 1986 the two began dating, and with Valerie living on her own, they moved in together.

As a personal assistant, Garces organized Williams's daily schedule. And as a mate, she helped him realize that he did not need blockbuster movies or the adulation of fans to feel successful. Combined with his sobriety and the birth of Zach, Garces's positive influence helped transform Williams into a more confident, stable individual.

His friends noticed an immediate difference in Williams. Pam Dawber said of Garces, "She's Robin's anchor. She's reality. Ground zero. She's very sane, and that's what he needs. She's incredibly loving, too. And protective. She knows who is bad for him and who is good, and she helps keep the good relationships going."[64]

A Contented Life

Once Garces entered his life, Williams seemed stronger and more content. His happiness translated into more successes onstage. During the late 1980s, he cohosted a series of comic performances called Comic Relief. In 1986 he and two close friends, fellow entertainers Billy Crystal and Whoopi Goldberg, organized the first of a series of telethons to raise money for the homeless.

Williams poses with Comic Relief cohosts, Billy Crystal and Whoopi Goldberg.

His most satisfying 1986 triumph came separately from Comic Relief, however. This performance occurred in New York City, the scene of his theatrical background. That year, Williams garnered rave reviews for an appearance at the Metropolitan Opera House. When first approached with the idea, he wondered if he had the confidence to perform at such a dignified location and if he had the talent to win over the New York audience. But Garces's encouragement helped dispel the doubts. He flew to New York and, even though he battled his usual case of nerves, put on what many observers called the finest live performance of his career.

Williams also started seeing a therapist that same year to find out why, if he enjoyed such immense successes, he did not seem completely satisfied with his life. The therapist helped him understand that Williams performed as a way of gaining other people's acceptance, of being liked, and as a way to avoid being alone, perhaps because he had spent so many hours by himself as a youth. As Williams rose in the entertainment world, he started to think that people only accepted him because he was funny. The therapist helped him realize that he could be loved for himself, that people could love him for who he was instead of for being the popular comedian. In an effort to focus on what was truly important, the therapist also recommended that Williams slow down and spend more time with his son.

A Close Couple

As time passed, Robin Williams and Marsha Garces grew closer as a couple. In 1986, with Valerie Velardi involved in her own relationship, the two unofficially separated (the couple legally separated the following year). This action tightened the bond between Williams and Garces.

Soon the two were inseparable, a fact that did not go unnoticed by the press. Unaware that the difficulties between Williams and Velardi predated the comedian's relationship with Garces, gossip columnists labeled Garces a marriage-wrecking nanny. In a hard-hitting February 22, 1988, article that painted Garces as

San Francisco Anchor

Reflecting his relaxed lifestyle and his dedication to family, Robin Williams has established a casual home life near San Francisco. As he explained in Andy Dougan's biography, *Robin Williams,* "I live there [San Francisco] because you really don't want to have to worry about your career constantly. I mean, parking lot attendants give you scripts in Los Angeles. In San Francisco people accept me as me, they know I've done movies, but that's just part of it. I can go to a bike shop and buy some weird bike and hang out and talk to bike messengers and then I can get on my bike and ride forty miles across the Golden Gate [Bridge] to some other place, to woods, and be totally alone, and that's wonderful."

a villain, *People* magazine wrote of Williams, "Having beaten alcohol and drugs, he's now entangled in a love affair with his son's nanny that has left his wife embittered—and Zachary, 4, in the middle."[65]

The magazine article bothered Williams, who had tried to explain to the reporter that he and Velardi faced problems long before he met Garces. When the magazine declined to convey that point, friends of Williams gathered in support of the comedian and refused to sit for interviews.

People magazine did not stand alone. Other publications besieged the comedian for their own sessions. When Williams did not comply, they often wrote their own stories, sometimes without checking on details and facts. Photographers jammed cameras in his face and chased after him when he stepped out in public, and gossip publications fabricated tales.

The experiences embittered Williams. He later said,

> I fantasize about destroying the yellow journals [gossip magazines]. . . . They write the most amazing stuff, using quotes from supposed friends about your personal life. Of course, the people I love and care about don't believe it; most people know it's nonsense. But my wife's grandparents, for example, don't realize right away that it's fiction.[66]

Williams and Garces ignored the tabloids long enough to finalize plans for marriage. In front of a select group of close friends,

Williams poses with his second wife, Marsha Garces, and their children at a ceremony honoring the actor with a star on the Hollywood Walk of Fame.

the two were married on April 30, 1989, at Lake Tahoe, California. Within two years the couple gave birth to two children, daughter Zelda on July 30, 1989, and son Cody on November 25, 1991.

The combination of Marsha Garces, a family, and the therapy sessions had a calming effect on Robin Williams. Armed with fresh confidence, he entered a new stage of his performing career, one that again catapulted him to the forefront of his industry.

Chapter 6

"Accomplished and Familiar as an Actor"

As ROBIN WILLIAMS'S personal life improved, his professional career shot to new heights. He had always been able to turn a live audience into hysterics with his wild humor, and he enjoyed success in television. But he had failed to connect in the movie industry. That changed with his next project, a film about a radio disc jockey in Vietnam.

A Perfect Vehicle

The idea for the movie originated with the real-life disc jockey, Adrian Cronauer. In the early 1960s Cronauer began hosting a radio program in Saigon, the capital city of then South Vietnam, to bring laughter and a touch of home to the American soldiers fighting in the Vietnam War. For one year he opened the show with his trademark greeting, "Good morning, Vietnam." He then used lighthearted banter, wild humor, improvisational skits, and current musical hits to entertain the soldiers. The show quickly became popular.

After Cronauer returned to the United States, he and a friend, Ben Moses, wrote a screenplay based on Cronauer's Vietnam experiences. In the course of shopping the idea around Hollywood, the script landed on the desk of Larry Brezner, Robin Williams's agent. During a visit to Brezner's office, the comedian noticed the script, took it home, and read it. He immediately called Brezner to say he wanted to act in the film.

Soon after, Jeffrey Katzenberg, chairman of Walt Disney Studios, read the script and concluded it would be the perfect vehicle for

Robin Williams. Cronauer seemed to be the military disc jockey equivalent to Williams, since both heavily employed improvisation. Katzenberg explained that the movie was "about a disc jockey who gets on the air and goes through four hours a day of improvisational entertainment, narration, news bulletins, introductions to records. And those parts would give Robin his chance to improvise." [67]

Williams eagerly jumped into the role. He also saw the part as the first opportunity in film to employ his razor-sharp wit, the talent that endeared him to audiences. His movie credentials had, to date, focused on dramatic roles lightened with a mild strain of humor, but nothing close to what audiences had grown to love from his nightclub act and his role as Mork. He would now have the chance to transfer that asset to film.

While delighted to be able to take such a step, Williams knew he faced a crucial moment in his professional life. Should this movie, a film that seemed tailor-made for him, fare poorly at the box office, his hopes for a Hollywood career could be permanently extinguished.

To prevent this from happening, director Barry Levinson intended to give his star all the freedom he needed, especially in the first half of the movie. In many scenes he told Williams to use the script as a guide and to say whatever came into his mind. In hopes of capturing the spontaneity that marked Williams's club appearances, Levinson also often turned on the cameras without telling Williams.

The movie, titled *Good Morning, Vietnam* after Cronauer's opening, offered the comedian more than a chance to highlight his comedic skills, though. In an attempt to show the changes that Vietnam imposed on the American military, the film turned more serious in its second half. Williams then had to display the dramatic skills he sharpened at Juilliard.

The First Oscar Nomination

The formula worked. When the film opened in December 1987, audiences howled with delight at the hilarious lines in the movie's first half. Then they sat absorbed with Williams's dramatic side as he showed how Cronauer's life was altered by events he wit-

Director Barry Levinson encouraged Williams to improvise during the filming of Good Morning, Vietnam.

nessed in Vietnam. Critics praised Williams, saying his "manic monologues are so uproarious that they carry the rest of the film."[68] And friends asked him why he waited so long to star in a movie that so perfectly suited his comedic talents. For the first time, Williams delivered what his audiences expected—comedy—while also exhibiting a deft dramatic side.

The movie grossed $124 million in the United States, more than the combined take for his first seven films. It also propelled Williams's name into Oscar contention. In early 1988 the Academy of Motion Picture Arts and Sciences honored him with a nomination for Best Actor. The nomination pitted Williams against several talented actors, including Michael Douglas and Jack Nicholson. Besides the tough competition, Williams battled the unspoken Hollywood bias against honoring comedians, particularly those with a television background, with Oscars. In the end, he did lose to Douglas, but Williams's reputation as a moneymaker and fine actor rose.

The performing community recognized Williams's work in the film in other ways, however. He received a Golden Globe Award for best actor in a musical or comedy, a Grammy Award for best comedy recording of the year (for the *Good Morning, Vietnam* sound track), and American Comedy Awards for funniest male performer of the year and for funniest actor in a motion picture. In the aftermath of his triumph, better scripts poured into Brezner's office, handing Williams the opportunity to star in more commercial hits.

His Father's Death

Events in his personal life tempered Williams's elation over *Good Morning, Vietnam*. In October 1987, shortly before the movie premiered, Williams's father died from cancer. The two had grown close in recent years, mainly because Williams better understood his father once he faced his own parental responsibilities with Zach. Watching his father battle such a debilitating disease sobered the comedian. "Everyone always thinks of their dad as invincible," he stated later, "and in the end here's this tiny creature, almost all bone."[69]

Williams's portrayal of irreverent disc jockey Adrian Cronauer in Good Morning, Vietnam *earned him his first Oscar nomination in 1988.*

Williams could not dwell on his father's passing for long, however. Another successful film, this time about a high school teacher, occupied his attention.

Carpe Diem

Williams tackled an entirely different character for his next movie role, English teacher John Keating in 1989's *Dead Poets Society*. Although the film did contain some humorous lines, it downplayed Williams's comedic talents and highlighted his ability to portray a serious, calm individual. In the movie the fictional teacher, Keating, attempts to show his high school students the importance of being themselves in life and pursuing their dreams. In the process he clashes with his superiors at the exclusive boys' preparatory school where he works and with his students' parents, who have carefully outlined their sons' careers for them.

Initially, Williams and director Peter Weir wondered if they should portray Keating as a fast-paced deliverer of humorous lines, as Williams had done with Adrian Cronauer. Ultimately, though, they decided the movie would be better served if Williams quietly settled into the background and allowed the students to occupy center stage. Weir wanted audiences to connect with Keating, not with Robin Williams. By having the actor play the teacher in a calm manner, he achieved that goal. In his first scene with the boys, for instance, Williams barely raises his voice above a whisper as he talks to them about life and dreams and introduces the movie's trademark phrase, carpe diem—seize the day.

Williams, who patterned Keating after his Country Day School history teacher and wrestling coach, John Campbell, loved playing Keating. He explained, "I like the point of the movie, of trying to find the passionate thing in your life, finding some sort of passion."[70] The film struck a chord with audiences as well, who were moved by the powerful message. *Dead Poets Society* accumulated $96 million in the United States and made such a splash internationally that theater owners in Japan kept the lights off for five minutes after the movie's tragic end, which includes the suicide of one student and Keating's dismissal, to allow audiences to compose themselves.

Throw It in the Garbage

John Campbell, the Country Day School teacher after whom Robin
Williams based much of his *Dead Poets Society* character, claimed that
his former student actually presented a tamer version of what he was
like in the classroom. In Andy Dougan's 1998 biography of Williams,
Campbell said of the film version teacher, "He tells the students to rip
out the pages in their books. I tell them to throw the whole thing in
the garbage."

*Williams plays an English instructor with an unorthodox teaching
style in* Dead Poets Society.

Williams registered impressive reviews for this role. These
proved he did not have to rely on humor to move audiences. The
Boston Globe concluded, "Williams extends and deepens his dramatic reach, then generously stands back and lets the ensemble
of young actors shine."[71]

For his role in *Dead Poets Society,* Williams earned a second
Academy Award nomination, again for best actor. Even though
he lost to Daniel Day-Lewis's portrayal in *My Left Foot,* Williams
gained even more respect in Hollywood as a serious actor. He had
failed to take home an Oscar statuette, in part because of his comedy and television background, but Williams moved closer to the
day when he would shatter that barrier.

Two More Successes

Williams enhanced his reputation with his next major movie, *Awakenings*. The film centered around Dr. Malcolm Sayer, whose character was based on the experiences of real-life Dr. Oliver Sacks. In the 1960s, at Beth Abraham Hospital in New York, Dr. Sacks treated patients who had lapsed into deep comas from an encephalitis epidemic that swept the nation from 1916 to 1927. The epidemic killed 1.5 million people, and the survivors lived in a catatonic state that required round-the-clock treatment. No physician had successfully unlocked their comas and restored them to normalcy. Relying on a drug called L-dopa, Dr. Sacks was able to bring a group of patients out of their comas temporarily.

The script immediately hooked Williams. He read it while traveling on an airplane and became so emotionally moved that a flight attendant asked if he was all right. Williams noticed similarities between the shy, real life Dr. Sacks and himself,

Williams tends to Robert De Niro in Awakenings. *Williams's portrayal of Dr. Malcolm Sayer cemented his credibility as a serious actor.*

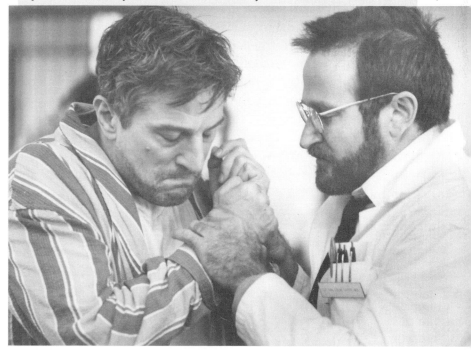

especially in relating to people. He recognized that Dr. Sacks forged relationships with his patients much like Williams used stand-up comedy to connect with audiences—it was easier for both to deal with people at the workplace rather than to open up on a one-to-one basis in a social setting. Williams agreed to take the role.

He tried to learn everything he could about Dr. Sacks and about the illness. By the time he acted his scenes, Williams so perfectly imitated Sacks's mannerisms that some of the physician's associates teased him that Dr. Sacks was imitating the comedian, not the other way around. His efforts made the 1990 film a success. It received an Academy Award nomination as best film (eventually losing to Kevin Costner's western epic, *Dances with Wolves*) and earned $52 million at the box office, vastly exceeding expectations.

Williams's performance in *Awakenings* also gained superb reviews and solidified the notion that he could perform in noncomedic roles. The *Wall Street Journal* claimed that Williams "has become so accomplished and familiar as an actor that it's no longer shocking to see him outside his manic stand-up comic persona." [72] Noted film critic Roger Ebert concluded Williams had turned in one of his finest performances.

The next year Williams followed with another triumph. He received his third Oscar nomination in five years for his acting in *The Fisher King,* the story of a homeless man who helps a radio personality. Pitted against some of Hollywood's finest actors for best actor—Robert De Niro, Nick Nolte, Anthony Hopkins, and Warren Beatty—Williams again lost the award, this time to Hopkins for *Silence of the Lambs*. But he added to his luster simply by being included among those talents.

Some Noted Failures

In between his moneymaking movies, Williams starred in other films. Some enjoyed moderate success; others fared poorly. *Cadillac Man,* for example, gained decent reviews in its 1990 run but failed to capture a sizable market. On the other hand, 1991's *Dead Again,* in which Williams played an angry psychiatrist in an unbilled role, did well.

Rough Movie Set

One scene in the 1990 movie *Awakenings* called for Robin Williams, as Dr. Malcolm Sayer, to restrain Leonard Lowe, the patient played by Robert De Niro. Lowe was reacting angrily, and Dr. Sayer had to calm him down. Instead of the scene unfolding according to the script, Williams knew something wrong had happened when he heard a loud crack. He soon realized that in their scuffle, he had accidentally broken De Niro's nose.

De Niro could have halted the scene and waited for treatment, but in the theatrical tradition of the show must go on, he continued acting. In that manner he would not have to worry about shooting the scene the next day, when his face would probably be swollen beyond recognition.

Williams wondered how De Niro would react following the incident. But the veteran actor held no grudge. The two continued to film the movie as if nothing had happened.

His most prominent failure of this period, however, occurred in a movie that seemed to offer everything—a famed director, outstanding stars, and a classic story. In 1991, director Steven Spielberg began work on the movie *Hook*. Based on the Walt Disney tale *Peter Pan,* the movie portrayed Peter Pan as an adult lawyer, played by Robin Williams, who returns to Neverland to save his children from Captain Hook, performed by Dustin Hoffman. When Julia Roberts joined the cast as Tinkerbell, all seemed in order for a smashing hit. To save costs during production, Spielberg, Hoffman, and Williams even deferred their salaries and agreed to split 40 percent of the film's theatrical, video, television, and merchandising profits.

Williams thought the movie's premise, which has the adult Peter Pan so busily engrossed in his work that he ignores his children, presented a powerful message. He believed it showed the preciousness of childhood and depicted as detrimental modern parents' tendency to put the demands of work above the needs of their children. "I believe childhood is a very precious time," he said, "and I don't want to miss it with my children because I did miss it with my father. He was out working all the time and was always off round the country. So I didn't get a chance to see him very much and I miss that."[73]

*Captain Hook (Dustin Hoffman) threatens an adult Peter Pan (Williams)
in* Hook.

Although the movie did all right at the box office, earning $117 million in the United States, the figures were far below Disney's hopes. In addition, the movie failed to create a sympathetic Peter Pan or an equally evil Captain Hook. This led many critics to wish for a return of the earlier version of Peter Pan. "If this is Peter Pan for the 90s," stated critic Leonard Maltin, "give us the 50s instead."[74]

Another disappointment came in the form of a role that Williams wanted but did not receive. He thought he had the role of the Joker wrapped up for *Batman*. But at the last minute, the producers offered it to Jack Nicholson. Apparently, Nicholson had been their choice all along, but when the noted actor was slow to decide to do the film, the producers turned to Robin Williams in an effort to prod Nicholson into accepting the role. The strategy worked, and Nicholson agreed to take the part. Williams came away disappointed, realizing that no matter who you were, in Hollywood a bigger star always received more consideration.

"The Best Stand-Up I Have Ever Seen"

Despite his growing success in films, Williams never abandoned his roots. Stand-up comedy before live audiences propelled him to stardom, so he regularly fit in concert performances and comedy tours between his movie roles. He enjoyed making unscheduled appearances at local comedy clubs to try out new material and to connect with an audience. To avoid overshadowing aspiring comics, who also wanted the stage, Williams usually headed to a club in the middle of a week or late at night, when the audiences were sparse. In that manner he avoided stepping on toes and creating resentment from newcomers.

No matter how long he might be away from a club, when Williams returned, he performed as if he had never been absent. Audiences responded with glee, knowing they were in for a treat. Dan Holzman, who acted as a warm-up act for Williams and for many other top comedians, stated, "Robin is definitely the best stand-up I have ever seen, out of all of them. Robin is the only one who I could stay and watch every night because he was always different." [75]

During his club appearances, Williams frequently asked organizers to place a large box of toys onstage, covered so that he did not know the box's contents. Williams then started his act by walking over to the box. As he pulled out each item, he launched into hilarious routines focusing on the toy. The razor-sharp wit that the comedian exhibited impressed even fellow performers. Barry Friedman, who also opened for Williams, explained,

> We have opened for everybody you can imagine, from Patti LaBelle to Jay Leno to Dean Martin to Tom Jones to Billy Crystal, and there is no other artist whose show I stayed to hear every single word of every night without exception. I just couldn't leave the theater when he was on stage. Nor could I change or take off my makeup. I just hung in the wings every night. [76]

As the 1990s continued, a mellower Robin Williams emerged. Confidence and contentment replaced insecurity and instability. Family matters, not work, occupied his attention. The change produced a slightly different person, one who could see his career for what it was and make choices accordingly.

Chapter 7

"He's Loved Even When He's Not Being Funny"

EMERGING FROM THE 1990s and moving into the new millennium, Williams could look back without regret on an amazing career. He had compiled a list of failures, to be sure, and had flirted dangerously with drugs, but his triumphs more than offset his setbacks. In fact, he would soon add that long-elusive trophy—an Oscar—to his showcase. The march to the Academy Award began with a remarkable movie in which he never showed his face but in which he dominated the action with his voice: 1992's *Aladdin*.

"Carte Blanche to Go Nuts"

Robin Williams agreed to do *Aladdin* because he thought his children would like it. He accepted a salary of seventy-five thousand dollars (low for someone used to making millions per film), but asked in return that Walt Disney not profit off his name or voice in any advertising or toy deals with fast-food restaurants. Disney agreed. Instead of first writing a script and drawing the characters, Disney's producers handed Williams a general idea of what his character, the genie, was doing and then asked Williams to record his improvised lines. Afterward, animators matched the genie's actions to what Williams had already recorded.

Williams headed into the studios with little idea of what he might say, but as he had so often done onstage, he had no trouble coming up with a wealth of hilarious material. If he found a collection of props placed in the studio by producers, Williams used them to create spur-of-the-moment routines. For one song, Williams impersonated Arnold Schwarzenegger, Jack Nicholson, a Scotsman, a dog, television host Ed Sullivan, and comedian Groucho Marx. Williams recorded more than thirty hours of entertainment for the producers, who could use only a small fraction for the two-hour film.

Williams loved the experience. He said, "I went into a room and started improvising, and these guys kept throwing ideas at

The genie offers Aladdin a wish in this scene from Walt Disney's 1992 animated film Aladdin.

The Amazing Personalities of Aladdin

One of Robin Williams's most remarkable performances occurred with 1992's animated classic, *Aladdin*. The comedian's imaginative mind gave life to fifty-two different characters and voices. Stephen Spignesi included the list in his 1997 book, *The Robin Williams Scrapbook*. The following were some of the characterizations:

Arnold Schwarzenegger
a Scotsman
a jive street guy
a surfer
a stewardess
a magician
a Roman centurion
a game show host
a goat
Jack Nicholson
a lightbulb
a submarine
a baseball pitcher
a Hawaiian tourist
a dragon
a comedian in Las Vegas
a dog
Ed Sullivan
Robert De Niro
Pinocchio
Maurice Chevalier
Arsenio Hall
a drum majorette
Rodney Dangerfield
a professor
a bumblebee
a one-man band
a pinball machine
Groucho Marx (noted American movie comedian)
cheerleaders

me. It just got wild. They let me play. That's why I loved it—it was like carte blanche [complete freedom] to go nuts."[77]

The film opened to glowing reviews and packed theaters. Both adults and children responded to the film's humor, which offered material that appealed to all ages. Some adults told Williams that they laughed so hard during the show that their children begged them to be quiet. Film critic Roger Ebert wrote, "Robin Williams and animation were born for one another, and in *Aladdin* they finally meet. Williams's speed of comic invention has always been too fast for flesh and blood; the way he flashes in and out of characters can be dizzying. In *Aladdin,* he's liberated at last, playing a genie who has complete freedom over his form—who can instantly be anybody or anything." [78]

Aladdin became Disney's most successful film. It earned $217 million in the United States and sold an astonishing 15 million copies in the first four weeks of video release. Williams, who wanted only to entertain his children, received a special Golden Globe Award in 1992 for his work in *Aladdin.*

Soon after the film's release, Disney broke their agreement with Williams by utilizing his voice as the genie in television ads to promote merchandise based on the film. As a result, the Aladdin sequel featured a different actor providing the genie's voice. However, by the time a third film was planned, Disney had apologized to Williams, put out a press release admitting to their error, and coaxed Williams back by giving him a Pablo Picasso painting worth an estimated $1 million. Williams returned as the genie for the third installment, *Aladdin and the King of Thieves.*

Mrs. Doubtfire

Williams's next two roles proved as unusual as any he had done. For the 1993 film *Mrs. Doubtfire,* Williams played an unemployed, divorced actor who dresses as a nanny called Mrs. Doubtfire so he can see more of his children. Both Williams and the movie's director, Chris Columbus, hoped that this film, centering on a divorced couple's desire to do what is best for their children, could show that good families can result even from awkward situations.

Williams again thoroughly prepared for the hilarious, yet sensitive, movie. With heavy makeup, wig, and fake breasts, he was unrecognizable even to those who knew him well. Costar Sally Field did not know who he was the first time she saw Williams made up as Mrs. Doubtfire. And his own son, Cody, two years old at the time he visited the set, failed to realize that he stood next to his father. Williams also liked to wander off the set in full

Williams (center) costars with Sally Field (far right) in the 1993 film Mrs. Doubtfire.

makeup, casually stroll into a store, and purchase items just to see the reaction of other people. No one knew that a famous actor stood in their midst.

For most of the film Columbus shot two takes, one that closely followed the script and another that allowed Williams to improvise. He then took the better performance from each and fashioned a movie that became one of the year's most lucrative films. When the movie crossed the $200 million mark, Williams posted the enviable record of working in two straight films that gained more than $200 million in ticket sales.

Some people criticized the film for its friendly portrayal of split families. Then vice president Dan Quayle claimed it negated family values and made a mockery of the standard family unit. Columbus and Williams heatedly denied those charges. Williams asserted that divorce affected more than half the families in the country and to ignore the issue was to insult all those children facing the dilemma. "We wanted kids to know that their family, if they came from a divorced family, was just as valid as the family next door with two parents. Also, it was important that kids seeing this picture knew it wasn't their fault just because their parents got divorced."[79]

Most of the nation agreed with the director and the movie star. Many people enjoyed the movie, and Williams again claimed an honor when he received the 1993 Golden Globe Award for best actor in a comedy.

"There Are Many Kinds of Families"

Three years later Williams took the part of Armand in the comedy *The Birdcage*. The film was about a homosexual nightclub owner whose straight son brings his fiancée and her ultraconservative family to meet his father. Because he had recently completed *Mrs. Doubtfire,* a movie that asked Williams to dress in drag, Williams passed on the film's main role of Albert [who also dresses in drag] to play the less flamboyant Armand. Williams willingly allowed fellow actor Nathan Lane, who played Albert, to grab the spotlight because he believed playing Armand would be better for his own career.

Williams (left) looks on while his partner Nathan Lane gets some bad news in the 1996 film The Birdcage.

Williams also chose the part because he felt that the movie addressed an important issue for society, that of bigotry against homosexuals and their families. He explained, "I grew up in San Francisco; I know many same-sex families. I tell people, 'They raise their children the same way you do–they love them. There are many kinds of families, not just the Norman Rockwell kind.'"[80]

Williams made the correct choice of roles. Audiences loved the chemistry between him and Lane, and the film took in $124 million in the United States alone.

With several successful films behind him, Williams stood at the pinnacle of success and was finally able to capture the gold statuette he had so long wanted. *Good Will Hunting,* which appeared in 1997, handed Williams the role of a lifetime. The actor/comedian made the most of this opportunity by giving a riveting performance as a psychiatrist haunted by his own demons. The role led to Williams stepping to the microphone as the winner of an Oscar.

Oscar's Half-Life

Besides starring in popular films and winning the Oscar for *Good Will Hunting,* Williams appeared in numerous other movies during the 1990s. Some did well. Others received lukewarm responses, but they showcased Williams's talents in diverse ways. These films also illustrated a pattern that typified the actor—he alternately starred in successful, then poor, then successful vehicles.

Some of the most interesting of these movies placed Williams in offbeat roles. *Being Human,* for example arrived in 1993 and required Williams to play five different characters named Hector who lived at varying times in history. The characters included a prehistoric man, a slave in ancient Rome, a medieval traveler, a shipwrecked sailor in Columbus's day, and a citizen in modern New York. The film made only a small profit, but critics praised Williams's performance.

He was not as fortunate for some of his other pre-Oscar films. *Toys* in 1992, *Jumanji* in 1995, *Jack* in 1996, and *Flubber* in 1997 added little to his reputation. But they did show a growing sensitivity in Williams—he accepted the roles mainly because his children asked him to or because he thought they would appeal to

Films Since *Good Will Hunting*

Robin Williams has made eight films since *Good Will Hunting*. Though none has earned him a second Oscar, he has delivered generally fine performances. He has kept true to his intention of accepting only roles that interest and challenge him. Ron Givens quotes Williams in his biography, *People Profiles: Robin Williams*. "My goal is just to keep doing as many interesting characters as possible. To be able to try as many different types of people as I can."

children. Rather than worry whether the movies would help his career, he thought of their effects on others, especially younger people.

As the 1990s wore on, Williams made several other films, although none matched the success of *Good Will Hunting*. He found that Oscar-caliber films were difficult to duplicate because, Williams claimed, the Oscar "had a half-life. The first day or two after you won it, everyone was: 'Hey, congratulations!' A week later, a couple of people: 'Hey, great!' Three weeks later: 'Didn't you . . . ?' Then a month later: 'Mork!'"[81]

Despite not starring in another Oscar winner, Williams compiled a list of solid films. In 1998, *Patch Adams*, with Williams in the lead role, introduced to audiences the unique Dr. Hunter D. "Patch" Adams, who employed humor to treat terminally ill patients. The next year Williams appeared in *Jakob the Liar*, a film about a Jew in Nazi-occupied Poland who tries to give hope to other condemned Jews trapped in the grip of the Holocaust.

Playing Dangerous Characters

By 2002, though, Williams asked his agent to locate films in which he could play more sinister characters. He wanted to avoid being typecast. Besides the brief role in *Dead Again*, he had rarely acted as an evil individual.

Three successive films in 2002—*Death to Smoochy, Insomnia*, and *One Hour Photo*—changed that. In the first, a dark look at the powers of television, Williams plays a popular television star who is suddenly replaced by a children's show anchored by a stuffed animal named Smoochy. Williams's character plans revenge for his ill fortune. The second film, one of his finest performances,

Williams plays a disturbed worker at a photo-processing counter in the 2002 film One Hour Photo.

pits Robin Williams as a murderer against a tough police officer played by Al Pacino. In the third, he plays a lonely worker at a one-hour photo stand who forms a macabre fantasy relationship with a family that brings its photos to him to develop.

"You Say, 'Why?'"

Though Williams continued to star in numerous film projects, he gradually expanded his work into other fields. He and wife

Marsha formed Blue Wolf Productions in order to have more control over Williams's projects. The two review scripts and then decide which of the many he will accept. Or they select the films they want to develop as producers.

Williams kept busy outside the industry as well. One year after *Mrs. Doubtfire,* Williams joined Robert De Niro and director Francis Ford Coppola in opening a San Francisco restaurant called Rubicon. He supported diverse charity causes, such as medical research into illness and injuries, raised money for the homeless, and collected funds for political candidates. Comic Relief, which he started with Billy Crystal and Whoopi Goldberg, passed the $50 million mark in total contributions.

Williams also worked to improve the arts and the physical education programs in schools. He contended that the government has cut important material from the educational curriculum, including an emphasis on the arts and physical development. In a magazine interview, he said, "We're raising a nation of overweight, unintelligent people. The cities have broken down, the educational systems suffer cutbacks."[82]

His most rewarding work comes when he gives something to children. He thus takes an active interest in the StarBright Foundation, which makes wishes come true for children dying from terminal diseases. The fact that youngsters have to face losing their lives is a sad reality that haunts Williams. He told a television reporter, "The thing that makes me sometimes feel that life is unfair, that flattens me, is when [I] see children with cancer. When you [think about] that, you say, 'Why?'"[83]

The Stars of Comic Relief

Robin Williams and his close friends, Billy Crystal and Whoopi Goldberg, are certainly most responsible for the success of Comic Relief through the years. But they have also had much assistance from other performers. Many top-named comedians have appeared to entertain Comic Relief audiences, thereby helping the project raise the millions that have gone to the homeless. The list contains many of the most famous names in entertainment. Among them are Jon Lovitz, Carl and Rob Reiner, Arsenio Hall, Michael Keaton, Jerry Lewis, Garry Shandling, Dennis Miller, Jim Carrey, Sharon Stone, Roseanne, Tom Arnold, Chris Rock, Dana Carvey, Sinbad, Martin Short, John Candy, and Howie Mandel.

"Robin, Help Me Here"

Although Williams has gained praise for his charity work, he has also earned high marks by being courteous to everyone and by letting his fans and fellow comedians know that he appreciates their support. Dan Holzman, who opened for some of Williams's comedy concerts, claimed that some entertainers ignore their warm-up acts, but not Williams. "A lot of them don't watch your show, and they don't want anything to do with you. But every night we could hear Robin laughing backstage. A lot of other guys take their role of being a celebrity a bit too seriously, but Robin was a lot of fun."[84]

Williams is equally gracious to fans. One time in Oregon, a girl approached him with the hope of obtaining an autograph. She became so nervous at the prospect of meeting her idol that she almost started crying. Instead of walking away, Williams gently chatted with her.

Dan Holzman remembered another instance when he and Williams stopped at a fast-food restaurant while driving to a performance. "Robin went in and everyone kind of freaked out. The manager came over and apologized but Robin said, 'Let me eat my meal, and then we can play around.' After he had finished his meal he stood up and did about fifteen or twenty minutes, he fooled around with the drive-in speaker, he did all this stuff just for the benefit of the folks in the restaurant. It was very cool."[85]

The way he treats fans is mirrored by his intense devotion to friends. He enjoys the companionship of a close circle of comrades, mostly from within the business. They know they can count on Williams if they need him.

When director Steven Spielberg was shooting the intense, masterful Holocaust drama *Schindler's List,* he became so distressed at watching some of the scenes that he could not shake them from his mind after leaving the set. Finally, he called Williams from Europe where he was filming the movie. Spielberg remembered, "Every day shooting *Schindler's List* was like waking up and going to hell. Twice in the production I called Robin Williams just to say, 'Robin, I haven't laughed in seven weeks. Help me here.' And Robin would do twenty minutes on the telephone."[86]

The most moving example of Robin Williams's concern for friends occurred with his treatment toward his longtime buddy, actor Christopher Reeve. On May 27, 1995, Reeve was paralyzed in a horse-riding accident. Reeve landed on his neck, cracking the first two vertebrae. He hovered between life and death for days in a Virginia hospital.

He eventually regained consciousness but faced a dangerous operation in which physicians had to reattach his neck to his spine. He later explained in his autobiography what ripped him out of his melancholy:

> As the day of the operation drew closer, it became more and more painful and frightening to contemplate. In spite of efforts to protect me from the truth, I already knew that I had only a fifty-fifty chance of surviving the surgery. I

Williams jokes with longtime friend Christopher Reeve. After a horse-riding accident left Reeve paralyzed, Williams helped his friend to cope by making him laugh.

lay on my back, frozen, unable to avoid thinking the darkest thoughts. Then, at an especially bleak moment, the door flew open and in hurried a squat fellow with a blue scrub hat and a yellow surgical gown and glasses, speaking in a Russian accent. He announced that he was my proctologist and that he had to examine me immediately. My first reaction was that either I was on way too many drugs or I was in fact brain damaged. But it was Robin Williams. He and his wife, Marsha, had materialized from who knows where. And for the first time since the accident, I laughed. My old friend had helped me know that somehow I was going to be okay.[87]

Williams has evidenced a growing maturity not only toward people but also toward the work he considers. Instead of taking on any project, he looks for characters that appeal to him or films that challenge him in new ways. Money no longer motivates Williams—he has accumulated enough to last his lifetime. Instead, he looks for something that hooks his attention and that he believes will entertain an audience.

"I'll Always Do Live Comedy"

With everything in order, the future looks bright for Robin Williams. He spends as much time as he can at his home near San Francisco. There he plays with his children and does things with his wife. He states that he will always perform, though, especially stand-up routines before live audiences. He says, "I'll always do live comedy, even if it should mean performing on the streets, with a little pig-nosed amp and a shitty microphone."[88]

There are differences, however, between Robin Williams today and the performer who first appeared in comedy clubs almost three decades ago. The most important is that he has come to understand that he does not need comedy or film success to be accepted. Audiences now exist for him to entertain, not as a way to gain validation. He has received that understanding by realizing his worth as an individual, a father, and a husband. As his wife, Marsha, says, "There are times now when he can relax enough to know he's loved even when he's not being funny."[89]

Notes

Introduction: "This Might Be the One Time I'm Speechless"

1. Quoted in Andy Dougan, *Robin Williams.* New York: Thunder's Mouth Press, 1998, pp. 229–30.
2. Quoted in Ron Givens, *Robin Williams: A Biography.* New York: Time, 1999, p. 8.
3. Quoted in Givens, *Robin Williams: A Biography,* p. 8.
4. Quoted in Jay David, *The Life and Humor of Robin Williams.* New York: Quill Books, 1999, p. 204.

Chapter 1: Comedy Was a Way of Connecting

5. Quoted in Givens, *Robin Williams: A Biography,* p. 13.
6. Quoted in Dougan, *Robin Williams,* p. 9.
7. Quoted in "Robin Williams," *Current Biography Yearbook, 1979,* CD-ROM. New York: H.W. Wilson, p. 1.
8. Quoted in Lawrence Linderman, "*Playboy* Interview: Robin Williams," *Playboy,* October 1982, p. 76.
9. Quoted in David, *The Life and Humor of Robin Williams,* p. 2.
10. Quoted in Linderman, "*Playboy* Interview: Robin Williams," pp. 76, 78.
11. Quoted in Dougan, *Robin Williams,* p. 13.
12. Quoted in David, *The Life and Humor of Robin Williams,* p. 3.
13. Quoted in Dougan, *Robin Williams,* p. 7.
14. Quoted in "Robin Williams," *Current Biography Yearbook, 1979,* p. 1.
15. Quoted in David, *The Life and Humor of Robin Williams,* p. 4.

16. Quoted in "Robin Williams," *Current Biography Yearbook, 1997*, CD-ROM. New York: H.W. Wilson, 1999, p. 1.

17. Quoted in Lawrence Grobel, "*Playboy* Interview: Robin Williams," *Playboy,* January 1992, p. 66.

18. Quoted in Linderman, "*Playboy* Interview: Robin Williams," p. 78.

19. Quoted in Givens, *Robin Williams: A Biography,* p. 17.

20. Quoted in Dougan, *Robin Williams,* p. 18.

21. Quoted in Linderman, "*Playboy* Interview: Robin Williams," p. 79.

Chapter 2: "This Kid Is Going to Make It"

22. Quoted in Dougan, *Robin Williams,* p. 24.

23. Quoted in David, *The Life and Humor of Robin Williams,* p. 9.

24. Quoted in Dougan, *Robin Williams,* p. 20.

25. Quoted in Dougan, *Robin Williams,* p. 21.

26. Quoted in Givens, *Robin Williams: A Biography,* p. 22.

27. Quoted in Givens, *Robin Williams: A Biography,* p. 23.

28. Quoted in Linderman, "*Playboy* Interview: Robin Williams," p. 83.

29. Quoted in Linderman, "*Playboy* Interview: Robin Williams," p. 85.

30. Quoted in Louise Bernikow, "The Right Role at Last," *Premiere,* January 1988, p. 41.

31. Quoted in Christopher Reeve, *Still Me.* New York: Random House, 1998, pp. 169–71.

32. Quoted in Dougan, *Robin Williams,* p. 230.

Chapter 3: "I Knew I Could Make These People Laugh"

33. Quoted in John Eskow, "Robin Williams: Full-Tilt Bozo," *Rolling Stone,* August 23, 1979, p. 43.

34. Quoted in David, *The Life and Humor of Robin Williams,* p. 46.

35. Quoted in Linderman, "*Playboy* Interview: Robin Williams," p. 73.

36. Quoted in Lisa Grunwald, "Robin Williams Has a Big Premise!" *Esquire,* June 1989, p. 120.

37. Quoted in Bernikow, "The Right Role at Last," p. 41.

38. Quoted in Dougan, *Robin Williams,* p. 38.

39. Quoted in Dougan, *Robin Williams*, p. 39.

40. Quoted in Givens, *Robin Williams: A Biography*, p. 32.

41. Quoted in Dougan, *Robin Williams*, p. 40.

42. Quoted in Eskow, "Robin Williams: Full-Tilt Bozo," p. 43.

43. Quoted in Linderman, "*Playboy* Interview: Robin Williams," p. 86.

44. Quoted in David, *The Life and Humor of Robin Williams*, p. 20.

Chapter 4: "I Am Mork from Ork"

45. Quoted in "Robin Williams," *Current Biography Yearbook, 1997*, p. 2.

46. Quoted in Dougan, *Robin Williams*, p. 53.

47. Quoted in Givens, *Robin Williams: A Biography*, p. 41.

48. Quoted in Dougan, *Robin Williams*, p. 60.

49. Quoted in "Robin Williams," *Current Biography Yearbook, 1997*, p. 2.

50. Quoted in Dougan, *Robin Williams*, p. 63.

51. Quoted in Eskow, "Robin Williams: Full-Tilt Bozo," p. 44.

52. Quoted in Dougan, *Robin Williams*, p. 70.

53. Quoted in Linderman, "*Playboy* Interview: Robin Williams," p. 70.

54. Quoted in Linderman, "*Playboy* Interview: Robin Williams," p. 70.

Chapter 5: The Deadly Sins of Hollywood Wait for Everyone

55. Quoted in Givens, *Robin Williams: A Biography*, pp. 51–52.

56. Quoted in Givens, *Robin Williams: A Biography*, p. 95.

57. Quoted in Givens, *Robin Williams: A Biography*, p. 68.

58. Quoted in Dougan, *Robin Williams*, p. 84.

59. Quoted in David, *The Life and Humor of Robin Williams*, p. 64.

60. Quoted in Bob Woodward, *Wired: The Short Life and Fast Times of John Belushi*. New York: Simon and Schuster, 1984, p. 398.

61. Quoted in Dougan, *Robin Williams*, p. 90.

62. Quoted in Stephen J. Spignesi, *The Robin Williams Scrapbook*. Secaucus, NJ: Citadel Press, 1997, p. 73.

63. Quoted in David, *The Life and Humor of Robin Williams*, p. 79.

64. Quoted in David, *The Life and Humor of Robin Williams*, p. 111.

65. Quoted in Dougan, *Robin Williams,* p. 144.

66. Quoted in Eskow, "Robin Williams: Full-Tilt Bozo," p. 43.

Chapter 6: "Accomplished and Familiar as an Actor"

67. Quoted in David, *The Life and Humor of Robin Williams,* p. 102.

68. Quoted in Spignesi, *The Robin Williams Scrapbook,* p. 110.

69. Quoted in Givens, *Robin Williams: A Biography,* p. 82.

70. Quoted in Spignesi, *The Robin Williams Scrapbook,* p. 115.

71 Quoted in Givens, *Robin Williams: A Biography,* p. 86.

72. Quoted in Givens, *Robin Williams: A Biography,* p. 93.

73. Quoted in Dougan, *Robin Williams,* p. 185.

74. Quoted in Spignesi, *The Robin Williams Scrapbook,* p. 131.

75. Quoted in Dougan, *Robin Williams,* p. 159.

76. Quoted in Spignesi, *The Robin Williams Scrapbook,* p. 21.

Chapter 7: "He's Loved Even When He's Not Being Funny"

77. Quoted in David, *The Life and Humor of Robin Williams,* p. 162.

78. Quoted in Spignesi, *The Robin Williams Scrapbook,* p. 137.

79. Quoted in David, *The Life and Humor of Robin Williams,* p. 178.

80. Quoted in David, *The Life and Humor of Robin Williams,* p. 185.

81. Quoted in Givens, *Robin Williams: A Biography,* p. 8.

82. Quoted in Grobel, "*Playboy* Interview: Robin Williams," p. 72.

83. Quoted in Spignesi, *The Robin Williams Scrapbook,* p. 70.

84. Quoted in Dougan, *Robin Williams,* p. 160.

85. Quoted in Dougan, *Robin Williams,* p. 160.

86. Quoted in Frank Sanello, *Spielberg.* Dallas: Taylor, 1996, p. 227.

87. Reeve, *Still Me,* p. 36.

88. Quoted in Linderman, "*Playboy* Interview: Robin Williams," p. 72.

89. Quoted in Givens, *Robin Williams: A Biography,* p. 94.

Important Dates in the Life of Robin Williams

1952

Robin McLaurim Williams is born in Chicago, Illinois, on July 21.

1968

The Williams family moves to Tiburon, California.

1969

Williams enrolls at Claremont Men's College.

1970

Williams enrolls at Marin Junior College.

1973

Williams wins a scholarship to attend Juilliard School in New York.

1975

Williams leaves Juilliard and returns to San Francisco, where he makes a splash in the comedy club circuit.

1976

Williams meets Valerie Velardi. Williams and Velardi leave San Francisco for Los Angeles. He makes his first appearances at Los Angeles comedy clubs, including The Comedy Store.

1977

George Schlatter, producer of *Laugh-In,* sees Williams perform at The Comedy Store and signs him as a member of the cast. Williams acts in the movie *Can I Do It . . . Till I Need Glasses?*

1978

Williams marries Valerie Velardi on June 4. He wins an audition to act as the alien, Mork, on *Happy Days*. The debut episode of *Mork and Mindy* is televised on September 14.

1979

Williams wins a Grammy for best comedy album for *Reality . . . What a Concept*. He wins a Golden Globe Award for best actor in a comedy series for *Mork and Mindy*.

1980

Williams acts in the movie *Popeye*.

1982

Williams acts in the movie *The World According to Garp*. Williams's friend, John Belushi, dies the night of March 5. The final episode of *Mork and Mindy* airs on June 10.

1983

Son Zachary is born in April. Williams acts in the movie *The Survivors*.

1984

Williams and his wife hire Marsha Garces as a nanny for Zachary. Williams acts in the movie *Moscow on the Hudson*.

1986

Williams and his good friends, Billy Crystal and Whoopi Goldberg, start Comic Relief. Williams performs at the New York Metropolitan Opera House. He acts in the movies *The Best of Times, Club Paradise,* and *Seize the Day*.

1987

Williams and his wife, Valerie, legally separate. Williams's father dies in October. He acts in the movie *Good Morning, Vietnam* and receives an Emmy Award for outstanding performance in a variety or musical program for "A Carol Burnett Special." Williams receives a Grammy Award for best comedy recording for *A Night at the Met*.

1988

Williams is nominated for an Academy Award for *Good Morning, Vietnam* and receives a Golden Globe Award for best actor in a musical or comedy for *Good Morning, Vietnam*. Williams receives an Emmy Award for outstanding performance in a variety or musical program for "ABC Presents a Royal Gala." He receives a Grammy Award for best comedy recording for *Good Morning, Vietnam,* and receives a Grammy Award for best children's recording for *Pecos Bill*.

1989

Williams marries Marsha Garces on April 30; daughter Zelda is born in July. Williams acts in the movies *The Adventures of Baron Munchhausen* and *Dead Poets Society*.

1990

Williams is nominated for an Academy Award for *Dead Poets Society*. He acts in the movies *Awakenings* and *Cadillac Man*.

1991

Son Cody is born in November. Williams acts in the movies *The Fisher King, Dead Again, Hook,* and *Shakes the Clown*.

1992

Williams is nominated for an Academy Award for *The Fisher King* and receives a Golden Globe Award for best actor in a musical or comedy for *The Fisher King*. Williams acts in the movies *Toys, Aladdin,* and *Ferngully . . . The Last Rain Forest*. He receives a Golden Globe Award for special achievement for *Aladdin*.

1993

Williams acts in the movies *Mrs. Doubtfire* and *Being Human*. He receives a Golden Globe Award for best actor in a comedy for *Mrs. Doubtfire*.

1995

Williams acts in the movies *Jumanji, Nine Months,* and *To Wong Foo, Thanks for Everything, Julie Newmar*. Williams's friend, Christopher Reeve, is paralyzed in a horse-riding accident.

1996

Williams acts in the movies *Jack, Hamlet, The Birdcage,* and *Joseph Conrad's The Secret Agent*.

1997

Williams acts in the movies *Good Will Hunting, Flubber,* and *Father's Day*.

1998

Williams receives an Academy Award as best supporting actor for *Good Will Hunting* on March 23. He acts in the movies *Patch Adams* and *What Dreams May Come*.

1999

Williams acts in the movies *Bicentennial Man* and *Jakob the Liar.*

2001

Williams acts in the movie *A.I.: Artificial Intelligence.*

2002

Williams acts in the movies *Death to Smoochy, Insomnia,* and *One Hour Photo.*

For Further Reading

Books

Margaret L. Finn, *Christopher Reeve: Actor and Activist*. Philadelphia: Chelsea House, 1997. This book, written for the teenage market, surveys Reeve's life and his bond with Robin Williams.

Adrian Havill, *Man of Steel*. New York: Signet, 1996. Havill's biography has some helpful information on the friendship between Reeve and Williams.

Anthony Holden, *The Oscars*. Boston: Little, Brown, 1993. The book has useful information relating to the background of the Academy Awards.

Leonard Maltin, *Leonard Maltin's Movie Encyclopedia*. New York: Plume Books, 1994. Maltin, a respected movie critic, compiles an excellent reference work containing biographies of more than two thousand actors and filmmakers.

Hal Marcovits, *Robin Williams*. Philadelphia: Chelsea House, 2000. Marcovits delivers a fine account of the comedian's life. Written for the junior high school market, the book helps provide basic details of Williams's rise to fame.

Walter Olesky, *Christopher Reeve*. San Diego: Lucent Books, 2000. Olesky delivers one of the finest biographies of Reeve for the teenage market. Readable and filled with detail, the book provides information on Reeve's friendship with Williams and how Williams helped him through his accident.

Thomas O'Neil, *The Emmys*. New York: Berkley, 2000. This volume offers almost anything a reader might want to know about the Emmy Awards, from a chapter on how winners are selected to best acceptance speeches. A valuable portion also outlines the general history of the awards.

Videotape

Robin Williams at the Actors' Studio. Produced by James Lipton in 2002, this is a sixty-minute interview with the comedian in front of a live audience consisting of drama students. The interviewer fails to ask in-depth questions, but the interview does at least draw out some interesting remarks and humorous lines from Robin Williams.

Websites

Christopher Reeve Paralysis Foundation (www.apacure.com). The official website of Williams's close friend, Christopher Reeve, contains personal information about the actor as well as much material on spinal injuries.

The Comedy Store (www.thecomedystore.com). This website contains material on renowned comedians who have appeared at The Comedy Store.

Hollywood.Com (http://hollywood.com). This site is helpful in locating basic information on movie stars.

The Juilliard School (www.juilliard.edu). This site, the school's official website, has much information on the famed school's history, its programs, and its distinguished alumni, including Robin Williams.

The Movie Times (http://the-movie-times.com). A collection of information about movies that includes short biographies of major stars.

Robin Williams (www.robinwilliams.com). This is the official website for Robin Williams.

Works Consulted

Books

Jay David, *The Life and Humor of Robin Williams*. New York: Quill Books, 1999. The author provides abundant detail about Williams's life, but a lack of organization may make it difficult for the reader to follow.

Andy Dougan, *Robin Williams*. New York: Thunder's Mouth Press, 1998. Dougan delivers a useful biography of the comedian/actor. He is especially good at describing the contributions that Williams's second wife made to his success.

Ron Givens, *Robin Williams: A Biography,* New York: Time, 1999. This biography, which obviously benefits from having the resources and material from *People* magazine at its disposal, is filled with relevant quotes from the entertainment industry. This is the most helpful of the three full-length biographies of the star.

Joseph McBride, *Steven Spielberg: A Biography*. New York: Simon and Schuster, 1997. McBride's book sheds light on the friendship between Robin Williams and Steven Spielberg.

Christopher Reeve, *Still Me*. New York: Random House, 1998. In addition to its uplifting spirit, Reeve's autobiography explains the deep friendship that developed between Reeve and Robin Williams, a bond that flowered with Williams's caring help after Reeve's serious accident.

Frank Sanello, *Spielberg*. Dallas: Taylor, 1996. Sanello's biography includes some helpful material on how Robin Williams assisted Spielberg while the famous director made *Schindler's List*.

Stephen J. Spignesi, *The Robin Williams Scrapbook*. Secaucus, NJ: Citadel Press, 1997. Movie fan Spignesi has assembled a wide-ranging and valuable book about Robin Williams that includes numerous photographs, script synopses of every *Mork and Mindy* episode, and summaries of various interviews Williams has granted.

Bob Woodward, *Wired: The Short Life and Fast Times of John Belushi*. New York: Simon and Schuster, 1984. This excellent biography of the late comedian has the most comprehensive account of Belushi's death found in print. It supports Robin Williams's statements that he had little to do with Belushi that evening other than spending ten minutes with him and sharing some cocaine.

Periodicals

Louise Bernikow, "The Right Role at Last," *Premiere,* January 1988. This article has some helpful information on Williams's drive to constantly perform.

John Eskow, "Robin Williams: Full-Tilt Bozo," *Rolling Stone,* August 23, 1979. Eskow's article reveals some interesting material about Williams's rise to fame and what fuels his comedic drive.

Lawrence Grobel, "*Playboy* Interview: Robin Williams, *Playboy,* January 1992. Though not as informative as the first *Playboy* interview conducted in 1982, this piece still has a few items of interest for the reader, especially Williams's views on Hollywood and media coverage of stars.

Lisa Grunwald, "Robin Williams Has a Big Premise!" *Esquire,* June 1989. This article, written after the comedian's bouts with drugs, contains helpful insights into what propels Williams.

Lawrence Linderman, "*Playboy* Interview: Robin Williams," *Playboy,* October 1982. Much of what appears in subsequent books or magazine articles about Robin Williams's childhood and rise to fame first appeared in this fascinating, lengthy interview. Williams divulged much information about himself in this incredible conversation.

"Robin Williams," *Biography Today, 1992 Annual Compilation*. Detroit: Omnigraphics, 1992. A good, brief overview of Williams's life.

"Robin Williams," *Current Biography Yearbook, 1979,* CD-ROM. New York: H.W. Wilson, 1999. A good, brief overview of Williams's life.

"Robin Williams," *UXL Biographies,* CD-ROM, 1996. A good, brief overview of Williams's life.

Internet Sources

Bruce Kirkland, "Pelican Stand-Off," *Toronto Sun,* December 10, 1995. www.canoe.ca. The brief article has helpful quotes about how Williams uses his comedy as a form of dealing with his fears.

J. Rentilly, "It's No More Mr. Nice But Slightly Annoying Guy for Robin Williams," *The Guardian,* September 28, 2002. http://film. guardian.co.uk. The brief article contains interesting information on Williams's three movie roles of 2002.

Index

"ABC Presents a Royal Gala" (television), 7
Academy Awards, 6–7
  Awakenings, 76
  Dead Poets Society, 74
  Good Morning, Vietnam, 70–71
  Good Will Hunting, 9–10, 86
Academy of Motion Picture Arts and Sciences, 71
Adams, Hunter D. "Patch" (character), 87
Affleck, Ben, 8, 10
Aladdin (animated film), 80–82
  Golden Globe for, 7, 83
Aladdin and the King of Thieves (animated film), 83
Altman, Robert, 54
American Broadcasting Company (ABC), 45
American Comedy Awards, 72
Amistad (film), 9
Archie Bunker's Place (television), 55
Armand (character), 85
Arnold, Tom, 89
As Good As It Gets (film), 9
Awakenings (film), 75–76
  accident on set of, 77
  Golden Globe for, 83

Batman (film), 78
Beatty, Warren, 76
Being Human (film), 86
Belushi, John, 61–62

Bernhard, Sandra, 38
Best of Times, The (film), 58
Beth Abraham Hospital (New York), 75
Beyond the Fringe (film), 28
Birdcage, The (film), 85–86
Bloomfield Hills, Michigan, 15
Blue Wolf Productions, 89
Boarding House, The (club), 34
Boogie Nights (film), 9
Boston Globe (newspaper)
  review of *Dead Poets Society,* 74
Boulder, Colorado, 47
Brezner, Larry, 43, 69
Bunker, Archie (character), 56

Cadillac Man (film), 76
Campbell, John, 73
  on Williams in *Dead Poets Society,* 74
Candy, John, 89
Can I Do It . . . Till I Need Glasses? (film), 53–54
Captain Hook (character), 77
Carl (pet turtle), 16
Carlin, George, 38
"Carol Burnett Special, A" (television), 7
Carrey, Jim, 38, 89
Carter, Tish, 60
Carvey, Dana, 89
Chaplin, Charlie, 6
Chase, Chevy, 59
Chicago, Illinois, 11–12

Claremont Men's College, 23
Club Paradise (film), 58–59
Columbus, Chris, 83
Comedy Store, The (club), 37–38
Comic Relief (telethon), 65, 89
Committee, The (improv group), 26
Coppola, Francis Ford, 89
Cora (pet parrot), 37
Cornell University, 29
Costner, Kevin, 76
Country Day School, 15
Cronauer, Adrian, 69
Crystal, Billy, 13, 79, 89
    Comic Relief and, 65
    as Academy Awards host, 10
Cunningham, Richie (character), 45

Damon, Matt, 8, 10
Damrosch, Frank, 30
Dances with Wolves (film), 76
Davis, Bette, 41, 52
Dawber, Pam, 47, 62
    on Marsha Garces, 64
Day-Lewis, Daniel, 74
Dayton Art Institute, 35
Dead Again (film), 76, 87
Dead Poets Society (film), 73
Death to Smoochy (film), 87
DeLuise, Dom, 44
De Niro, Robert
    in *Awakenings,* 75–76
    accident while filming
        Awakenings, 77
    John Belushi and, 61
    restaurant business and, 89
Detroit, Michigan, 15
Disney, Walt, 77
Dougan, Andy, 56, 74
    on being the new kid, 20
    on honesty of children, 58
Douglas, Michael, 71
Duke (pet dog), 16
Dunn, James, 25, 27

Ebert, Roger
    review of *Awakenings,* 76

Emmy Awards, 6-7
Eskow, John
    on Williams's style, 49
Esquire (magazine), 18

Fernwood 2 Night (television), 42
Field, Sally, 83
Fisher King, The (film) 7, 76
Flubber (film), 86
Fonz (character), 45
Ford Motor Company, 11, 15
Friedman, Barry
    on Williams's talent as stand-up
        comedian, 79

Garces, Marsha
    growth of relationship with,
        66–67
    see also Williams, Marsha
Garp, T.S. (character), 58
Givens, Ron, on Williams's career
    after *Good Will Hunting,* 87
Gloaming, In the (film), 29
Goldberg, Whoopi, 38, 65, 89
Golden Apple Award, 51
Golden Globe Awards, 6
    Aladdin, 83
    Awakenings, 83
    Boogie Nights, 9
    Fisher King, The, 7, 76
    Good Morning, Vietnam, 7, 72
    Mork and Mindy, 52
    Mrs. Doubtfire, 85
Good Morning, Vietnam (film), 70–71
    sound track for, 7, 72
Good Will Hunting (film), 7, 87
    Academy Award for, 8–9, 86
    Screen Actors' Guild Award for,
        9
Grammy Awards, 6–7, 87
    Reality . . . What a Concept
        (album), 51
Grunwald, Lisa
    on origins of Williams's comedy,
        18

Hall, Arsenio, 38, 89
Happy Days (television), 44, 45

Harper, James
  on Williams at Marin College,
    26
Harvey Lembeck Comedy
  Workshop, 38
Haynes, Marjorie, 11
Hepburn, Katharine, 29
Hill, George Roy, 57
Hitchcock, Alfred, 29
Hoffman, Dustin, 77
Hollywood, California, 52
Holy City Zoo (club), 34
Holzman, Dan
  on opening for Williams, 90
  on Williams as stand-up
    comedian, 79
Hook (film), 77–78
Hopkins, Anthony, 9, 76
Houseman, John, 28, 31
Howard, Ron, 44–45

Idle, Eric, on Williams's reaction to
  cancellation of *Mork and Mindy,*
  56
Improv, The (club), 38
Inherit the Wind (film), 47
Insomnia (film), 87
Institute of Musical Art, 30
Intersection, The (club), 33

Jack (film), 86
Jack Paar Show, The (television), 35
Jakob the Liar (film), 87
Joker (character), 78
Jones, Tom, 79
Juilliard, Augustus D., 30
Juilliard School, 27
  history of, 30
Jumanji (film), 86

Katzenberg, Jeffrey, 69
Keating, John (character), 73
Keaton, Michael, 89
Kentfield, California, 25
Kinnear, Greg, 9
Knowles, John, 27

LaBelle, Patti, 79

Lake Tahoe, California, 68
Lane, Nathan, 85
Laugh-In (television), 40
Lembeck, Harvey, 38
Leno, Jay, 79
Letterman, David, 38
Levinson, Barry, 7–10, 71
Lewis, Jerry, 89
Linderman, Lawrence
  on Williams and his dog, 15
  on sensitivity of Williams, 51
"Lord Stokesbury, Viceroy of
  India." *See* Williams, Robert
  Fitzgerald
Los Angeles, California, 27
Lovitz, Jon, 89
Lowe, Leonard (character), 77

Magna Cum Laude Society, 19–20
Maltin, Leonard
  review of *Hook,* 78
Mandel, Howie, 89
Marin Junior College, 25
Marshall, Garry, 44
Martin, Dean, 79
Martin, Steve, 59
Marx, Groucho, 81
Matawaran, Lorenzo, 33
Matter of Gravity, A (film), 29
Metropolitan Opera House, 66
Miller, Dennis, 89
Milwaukee, Wisconsin, 45
Moore, Dudley, 28
Mork and Mindy, 47
  cancellation of, 55–56
  Golden Globe for, 7, 52
  network censors and, 49–50
  universal appeal of, 50
Mork from Ork (character), 44
Moscow on the Hudson (film), 58
Moses, Ben, 69
Mrs. Doubtfire (film)
  controversy and, 85
  costuming for, 83–84
  Golden Globe for, 7
Mull, Martin, 42
Murphy, Eddie, 38, 59
Murray, Bill, 59

My Left Foot (film), 74

Napa Valley, California, 52
Newsweek (magazine)
   review of *Moscow on the Hudson,*
   58
New York City, 27–28, 30
New York Metropolitan Museum
   of Art, 29
Nicholson, Jack, 71, 81
   as the Joker, 78
Night at the Met, A (recording), 7
Nolte, Nick, 76

One Hour Photo (film), 87
On the Waterfront (film), 51
Oscar. *See* Academy Awards

Pacino, Al, 88
Paris, Jerry, 45
Patch Adams (film), 87
Pecos Bill (children's recording), 7
People (magazine)
   reports of Williams's love life, 67
People Profiles: Robin Williams
   (Givens), 87
Perry Mason (television), 47
Peter Pan (character), 77
Pink Panther (film), 34
Playboy (magazine), 15, 51, 77
Popeye (character), 54
Popeye (film), 57
   failure of, 56
Price, Leontyne, 30
Princeton, 20
Pryor, Richard, 38

Quayle, Dan, 84

Reality . . . What a Concept
   (album), 51
   Grammy for, 7
Rear Window (television
   miniseries), 29
Redwood High (California), 21
Reeve, Christopher, 29
   at Juilliard, 28
   roles played by, 54

Williams's encouragement for,
   91–92
on Williams's experience at
   Juilliard, 31
Reiner, Carl, 89
Reiner, Rob, 89
Reynolds, Burt, 9
Richard Pryor Show, The (television),
   41–42
Ritter, John, 38
Roberts, Julia, 77
Robin on the River (Haynes), 11
Robin Williams (Dougan), 20, 56,
   58, 67, 74
Robin Williams Scrapbook, The
   (Spignesi), 82
Rock, Chris, 89
Rodriguez, Paul, 38
Rolling Stone (magazine), 49
Roseanne, 38, 89
Rubicon (restaurant), 89

Sacks, Oliver, 75
Saigon (South Vietnam), 69
Salamander, The (club), 34
San Francisco, California
   comedy community in, 21
   home in, 67
   theater community in, 32
Saturday Night Live (television), 40,
   51, 61
Saved by the Bell (television), 48
Sayer, Malcolm (character), 75
Schindler's List (film), 90
Schlatter, George, 39–41
Schwarzenegger, Arnold, 81, 82
Screen Actors' Guild Award, 9
Sellers, Peter, 34
Separate Peace, A (Knowles), 27
Shakespeare, William, 27
Shandling, Garry, 38, 89
Shore, Pauly, 38
Short, Martin, 89
Silence of the Lambs (film), 76
Sinbad, 89
Smith, McLaurin, 14
Smithsonian Museum of American
   History, 45

Somewhere in Time (film), 29
Spielberg, Steven, 77, 90
Spignesi, Stephen J.
    list of characters imitated in
        Aladdin, 82
    on Williams's children and fail-
        ure, 58
StarBright Foundation, 89
Steve Allen Show, The (television), 35
Still Me (television film), 29
Stone, Sharon, 89
Sullivan, Ed, 81
Superman (film), 28, 29, 54
Survivors, The (film), 58
Synergy Trust, The (improv
    group), 24

Taylor, James, 30
Three's Company (television), 38–39
Tiburon, California, 20
Tinkerbell (character), 77
Tonight Show, The (television), 35
Topanga Canyon, California, 52
Toys (film), 58, 86
Tramer, Bennett
    on Williams's reaction to fans, 48
Twelfth Night (Shakespeare), 27

United Artists, 44

Velardi, Valerie, 35–37
    marriage to, 43
    separation and divorce from,
        66–67

Wall Street Journal (newspaper)
    review of *Awakenings,* 76
Walt Disney Studios, 69
Wayans, Damon, 38
Weir, Peter, 73
Welch, Raquel, 56
Williams, Cody, 68, 83
Williams, Laurie, 13–14

Williams, Marsha, 10
Williams, Robert Fitzgerald, 10–11
    death of, 72–73
Williams, Robin McLaurim
    awards of, 6
    birth of, 11
    charity and, 53, 89–90
    children and, 86
    comedy, dealing with life and,
        34–35
    dating and, 24, 32–33
    drugs and, 21–22, 62–63
    evil characters played by, 87
    fans and, 90
    on homosexuality and bigotry,
        86
    inner fortitude of, 30
    lawsuit against, 60
    marriages of, 36, 43, 68
    as mime, 29
    mimicry and, 17–18
    playing a man-child, 47
    relationship with father of,
        10–12, 72–73
    relationship with mother of,
        13–14
    restaurant business and, 89
    school and, 14–16, 19–20, 22
    sports and, 18–19
    study of politics by, 23
    therapy and, 66
    womanizing by, 60
Williams, Todd, 14
Williams, Zachary, 63–64
Williams, Zelda, 68
Winkler, Henry, 44, 45
Winters, Jonathan, 34–35, 50
    Happy Days and, 44
    on *Mork and Mindy,* 56
World According to Garp, The (film),
    57–58

Yo-Yo Ma, 30

Picture Credits

Cover photo: Hubert Boesl/DPA/Landov
AP/Wide World Photos, 36, 53
© Bettmann/CORBIS, 31, 42, 59
CBS/Landov, 35
Jeff Christensen/Reuters/Landov, 65
© CORBIS SYGMA, 9
Courtesy James Dunn, 26
© Duomo/CORBIS, 19
Getty Images, 12, 22, 40, 63, 85
© A. Grace/CORBIS SYGMA, 91
Gary Hershorn/Reuters/Landov, 10
Hulton/Archive by Getty Images, 54
© Henry Grossman/Time Life Pictures/Getty Images, 25
Brendan McDermid/Reuters/Landov, 13
Ethan Miller/Reuters/Landov, 71
Wynn Miller/Time Life Pictures/Getty Images, 39
© Ohlinger Jerry/CORBIS SYGMA, 29
Photofest, 46, 48, 50, 61, 72, 74, 75, 78, 81, 88
Rose Prouser/Reuters/Landov, 68
© rien/CORBIS SYGMA, 84
© Royalty-Free/CORBIS, 16

About the Author

John F. Wukovits is a junior high school teacher and writer from Trenton, Michigan, who specializes in history and biography. Besides biographies of Anne Frank, Jim Carrey, Michael J. Fox, Stephen King, and Martin Luther King Jr. for Lucent Books, he has written biographies of the World War II commander Admiral Clifton Sprague, Barry Sanders, Tim Allen, Jack Nicklaus, Vince Lombardi, and Wyatt Earp. He is also the author of many books about World War II, including *Pacific Alamo: The Battle for Wake Island*. A graduate of the University of Notre Dame, Wukovits is the father of three daughters—Amy, Julie, and Karen.

DATE DUE